Run Your FIRM Like a BUSINESS

An Operations Guide for the Solo Practitioner and Small Law Firm

D1829194

Frank T. Lockwood

ABA
AMERICAN BAR ASSOCIATION
Solo, Small Firm and
General Practice Division

Cover design by Bobbie Sanchez/ABA Publishing.

The materials contained herein represent the opinions of the authors and/or the editors, and should not be construed to be the views or opinions of the law firms or companies with whom such persons are in partnership with, associated with, or employed by, nor of the American Bar Association or the General Practice, Solo and Small Firm Division unless adopted pursuant to the bylaws of the Association.

Nothing contained in this book is to be considered as the rendering of legal advice for specific cases, and readers are responsible for obtaining such advice from their own legal counsel. This book is intended for educational and informational purposes only.

© 2013 Frank T. Lockwood. All rights reserved.

No part of this publication may be reproduced, stored in a retrieval system, or transmitted in any form or by any means, electronic, mechanical, photocopying, recording, or otherwise, without the prior written permission of the publisher. For permission contact the ABA Copyrights & Contracts Department, copyright@americanbar.org, or complete the online form at http://www.americanbar.org/utility/reprint/html.

Printed in the United States of America.

17 16 15 14   5 4 3 2

CIP Data is on file with the Library of Congress.

Discounts are available for books ordered in bulk. Special consideration is given to state bars, CLE programs, and other bar-related organizations. Inquire at Book Publishing, ABA Publishing, American Bar Association, 321 N. Clark Street, Chicago, Illinois 60654-7598.

www.ShopABA.org

CONTENTS

INTRODUCTION

Is This Book for You?

If the tension between the actual practice of law and the administrative or business demands seems never ending, this guide is for you.

It is not easy to run a successful small law firm *and* be an effective lawyer. You frequently need to resolve the tension between the *shoulds* of timely billing, reviewing financial statements and cash flow, motivating employees, managing your cases, and actually doing the legal work for which you were trained. You are also aware of desirable business practices in such areas as human resources and marketing, for example, but you never seem to have enough time to address them, let alone implement them. By definition, your case deadlines always take precedence over those administrative headaches or desires. That is, until one of your employees quits without notice, or worse, you cannot meet payroll. Then and only then do you instantly become a firefighter and put out the cash flow or employee fire. The problem is, these fires typically arise when you can least address them. But you have no choice. Or do you?

Most attorneys hate the administrative part of the profession and avoid it until they are forced to face it. This is absolutely the wrong way to run a law firm.

This perspective will result in the continual sacrifice of your peace of mind, and it will cause you and others ongoing stress. How do you balance these competing demands—especially when your client deadlines are immovable and seem to follow one after the other with little room in between? Wouldn't it be nice to plan your business strategy like you plan your case strategy? Without big-firm bureaucracy or expense, how do you avoid those small-firm problems like irregular cash flow, employee turnover, increasing accounts receivable, and collection challenges that seem to recur?

The answers to these questions are contained in this book.

The systems described in this guide took years to develop and refine to reach the proper balance between what I previously had considered competing demands on my time. Before that, I had felt that investing more time into my cases might produce better results for my clients. And while this may have been true, I was falling behind on the business and administrative demands of my own firm.

I couldn't do both effectively, could I?

Every time I encountered a problem that caused cash flow, employee, or collections challenges, for example, I began to realize that the decision-making process that got me into these messes was either nonexistent, flawed, or needed tweaking to avoid repeating the same problem.

I had to ask myself: *What was the decision (or lack thereof) I had made before this happened that created this problem?* Once I was honest with myself, or was helped to be honest by trusted staff or my spouse, I could identify the source of the problem and implement a policy or procedure that would prevent it from happening again, or at least reduce the likelihood of it happening again. I also realized that I didn't have to reinvent the wheel when doing this. I could adopt systems or procedures used by other small firms that had worked for them.

For example, if I had a cash flow problem and had to borrow money from my line of credit, I looked into the past month's work and tried to identify why all these hardworking employees (lawyers and legal assistants) did not produce enough revenue to cover our overhead. Sometimes the answer was that we were working on a case for which we wouldn't get paid until sometime in the future. Maybe we were waiting for the sale of an asset or a court ruling.

Or perhaps, the problem was much less specific and more common. For example, frequently we had depleted the retainers for several clients and had failed to call them to request replenishment of those retainers. Many times we had just continued working on a case or for a client who had stopped paying us long ago, and we either never noticed or even asked why. I ultimately realized that without someone (1) whose job description specifically called for them to keep an eye on retainers, and (2) whose calendar included scheduled calls to clients *every billing cycle* to get the retainers replenished, and (3) who reported to and met with the managing partner *every billing cycle* to make a decision as to the future handling of the case, we were bound to experience cash flow challenges again and again.

Once a problem arises, it's already too late to change a policy or procedure that will address that particular problem. One can, however, make systemic policy or procedural changes to prevent this problem from recurring. These changes must be the result of carefully thinking one's way through how each decision (or lack thereof) either supports or sabotages a good business practice or goal of the firm.

There is rarely a middle ground. Whether it's a decision to accept a case or hire a specific employee, or any number of seemingly unimportant decisions during the life of the case, each decision or policy has a predictable result.

Without a system to guide your practice, it will be hard to avoid problems and work your way out of the morass you have created by practicing law ad hoc.

I found that creating and sticking to a system in each area of practice prevented most problems from recurring. Once carefully designed and implemented, these systems changed the nature of my practice and the attitude of every employee in my firm—including me—for the better.

I discovered that there is a symbiotic relationship between the pure practice of law and the administrative functions of planning for and running a law firm. That is, as the proper planning and systems were implemented, the pure practice of law could be addressed with much less stress, and it usually resulted in much more profit. This was great news!

This guide, then, seeks to achieve the proper balance between and successful integration of these two worlds. Based on thirty years of law practice, from the perspective of both an employee and an owner/employer, this book identifies various areas where solo practitioners or small law firms typically fall short in valuing and systematizing the administrative areas of running a law practice—and where unclear, unconscious (or even improper) individual goals can sabotage long-term growth and success of the entire firm.

This guide is all about systems: how to design them, implement them, and stick to them. It will revolutionize your practice. Once various elements of these systems are implemented, common, recurring problems such as increasing accounts receivables and employee turnover are minimized. Stress is decreased, while profits increase, and satisfied clients abound. *It is important to note that you may not have the personnel available to implement every aspect of every system recommended in this guide. That is okay. Every time you implement just one small element, your practice will improve in a measurable way.*

I divided the practice into several areas that could stand by themselves and for which changes could be implemented in varying degrees. Areas such as case management, timekeeping and billing, and human resources are traditional areas that needed addressing—and in my experience systematizing— so they can be conquered once and for all.

Although it is complete with forms useful to family law practice (which was my specialty), many of the forms can be adapted to fit your area of practice. I also anticipate that future editions will include specific forms that can be used for different areas of practice.

The timekeeping and billing chapter is adaptable for a practice of any size in any area that bills by the hour. If adopted, it should dramatically catapult your firm's profitability, which will have a profound impact on the hours you work, the amount you are able to pay your employees, and the overall success of your firm. It can turn a struggling practice into a thriving, vital enterprise with benefits for employees and owners alike.

I am also sure that some of you reading this book may already have portions of your practice systematized to a point that works well for you. That's great. You may want to ignore those portions of this book that don't seem to apply to your firm's systems, but I recommend you read the chapters anyway. You might pick up a useful tip or two to incorporate into your firm's current system or learn how another firm handles these portions.

Finally, it should be noted that this book assumes that you already have a going concern and you desire to improve it. Hence, it is not really a book for start-ups. For those of you who are really starting from scratch and have no idea where to place your computer or photos on your desk, or what your hourly rate should be, I recommend Jay Foonberg's *How to Start and Build a Law Practice.* He helped me thirty years ago when I was starting out and dreaming of someday owning my own practice. In its fifth edition as of this writing, it remains an outstanding and comprehensive tome for those contemplating starting and building a private practice.

1

HOW TO DESIGN AN EFFECTIVE INFORMATION MANAGEMENT SYSTEM

There are three ways that relevant information enters your law firm: (1) by voice, usually telephone or voice mail, (2) by hard copy, usually by mail or hand delivery of documents, and (3) digitally, usually by e-mail or, to a much lesser degree, by fax. How well or poorly each of these types of information is handled can invigorate (or hamper) the effectiveness, efficiency, profitability, and growth of your firm's practice.

Telephone Calls

The Initial Telephone Call (Intake)

The Problem: Old-School Ways of Answering the Telephone.

Calling a law firm for the first time usually brings one of two results for the caller:

1. The caller hears "I will have a lawyer call you back just as soon as one is available," which means that the caller usually contacts and retains another firm before the call-back even occurs.
2. The caller actually speaks to an attorney who is sensitive about the free time he or she is giving away on the phone, so the attorney is too curt or brief to allow the caller or the attorney a proper environment in which to make an informed decision about whether to move forward in a business relationship.

Once an attorney starts down that road of giving free advice on the phone (and you all know exactly what I am talking about), it's difficult to transition to setting an appointment. If you don't give enough advice, or need to be abrupt, the caller feels cheated. If you answer every question from the caller, taking forty-five minutes or an hour, the caller has no incentive to come in for an appointment. The caller thinks that he or she has a clear picture of the case and how to proceed (which the caller doesn't). The caller has no idea who you or your firm are and how you operate. You have no real idea who the caller is or whether you have gathered enough information to provide dependable, responsible legal advice. You've made no headway towards securing a well-paying client.

It is almost impossible for an attorney to give responsible or accurate advice after talking for only a few minutes on the telephone. You cannot get a complete picture of the entire case that way. Providing legal advice on anything less than complete information is downright irresponsible.

Answering calls from unknown people and walking the tightrope between good marketing and sound legal practice place any attorney in an untenable position. The attorney must constantly choose between giving away dozens of free, unscheduled hours of time each month to callers who are not even clients, or being ever so brief so the lawyer can get back to working for the paying clients. Some firms rotate this task among their attorneys. The associates usually resent the work of selling legal services for their bosses, who aren't going to share the firm profits with the associate: "Why should I do this when I am being evaluated only by my billable hours anyway?" In conclusion: the traditional system of attorneys giving advice over the phone to first-time callers is actually counterproductive and has almost never proven effective.

One final nail in this coffin: If an attorney gives away .75 hours every *other* day to a first-time caller, for example, that's equivalent to about 7.5 hours per month not billed. At $250 per hour, that's a loss of $1,875 per month *for each attorney* in the firm. That's a lot of lost revenue for a system that doesn't really work.

I don't care how sophisticated your voice-mail system is, it won't solve your problem either. People in distress do not want to hear a recording, nor can they figure out how to navigate your voice-mail system. Rather, they want a courteous, caring, and competent voice at the other end of the phone to assist them.

Does this mean that first-time callers must talk to a lawyer and get free advice?

Of course not.

Does it mean that the caller must be satisfied leaving a message and then waiting by the phone for who knows how long before they get a return call?

Clearly not.

The Solution: Upgrade the Receptionist Position

Once I realized that I needed to develop a system of handling calls from potential clients that fell somewhere between these two extremes, I realized that the traditional receptionist position still used in most law firms was simply outdated. I struggled, experimented, and tested various methods of handling those first calls. I actually installed a "sophisticated" voice-mail system that initially answered every telephone call. It was too sophisticated, apparently. I received so much negative feedback that I pulled it within two weeks. *So much for a high-tech telephone system,* I thought.

What I finally realized was that I needed a skilled, non-attorney answering the phone who could elicit specific information from callers without giving free legal advice. This person had to be someone who could move the caller from casual information seeker to potential client. Or—equally as important—the person had to be someone who could disqualify the caller as a client. That kind of person needed to be much more than a traditional receptionist. That person needed specific training on the entire process of moving a client from a telephone intake process to an in-office consultation or from an initial phone call to a rejection. I ended up calling this person my intake coordinator, as this person was ultimately put in charge of coordinating and directing all communications from outside the office to the intended recipient within the office.

Once the intake coordinator (coordinator) determines that a new caller is on the line, the coordinator must perform a conflict check of the caller and any opposing or related parties to the caller's case. The coordinator simply asks the caller to hold for a minute to make sure our firm does not have a conflict. If your firm has a comprehensive contact manager or address book on its server, this can be accomplished within seconds. If the caller's name, spouse's name, or any other name mentioned by the caller appears in our contact manager, the coordinator tells the caller that that there may be a problem without disclosing what the problem may be. The coordinator explains the need to check with an attorney and get back to the caller before we can proceed. Not one substantive question or answer should pass between the coordinator and the caller before this is accomplished. Otherwise, the firm is exposed to being disqualified from representing the caller, or worse, from representing a current client of the firm. There are savvy folks who know how to game the system. They call dozens of firms, never intending on hiring them, but rather seeking to disqualify the firm from representing their spouse or an opposing party. I have won many motions seeking to disqualify our firm on the basis of a conflict due to our good record keeping and by demonstrating that the caller telephoned several firms for the sole purpose of preventing the opposing party from hiring a good attorney.

If there is no conflict, the coordinator checks the box on the telephone intake form (see Appendix 1) to indicate that the coordinator has performed the conflict check.

Next, the coordinator must determine if the caller and the case is the type your firm handles. It is good practice to have a system of collecting information to evaluate whether this client and the case fit into your firm's practice profile. The process serves to move the caller forward to an initial consultation for which the caller pays. It also provides many points at which the client may disqualify himself or herself by refusing to follow your system. In other words, if the client does not want to wait for an in-office consultation, or does not want to pay for it, or insists on free advice immediately, the caller disqualifies himself or herself from becoming a client of your firm.

Over time through trial and error, and after some focused brainstorming sessions, I developed a script or outline of questions that my coordinator asks the caller. First, the coordinator seeks permission to ask a few questions about the caller's situation.[1] If the caller consents, and almost all do, the coordinator follows this script, and fills in the form with the caller's answers (see Appendix 1). If the coordinator feels confident that the caller's situation is the kind the firm handles, then the coordinator tells the client that he or she should come into our office for a full legal consultation with an attorney. This consultation would answer all of the caller's questions and concerns and provide preliminary feedback on the merits of their case. The use of a script by a trained person eliminates the need for a lawyer to be available for a new caller, and it can prevent the loss of thousands of hours of billable time over the life of the lawyer's career. It also serves to avoid the no-win situations described above while providing the caller with an intelligent connection with the firm until he or she can meet an attorney and retain the firm.

The coordinator then sets an appointment for the potential client[2] and informs him or her that some financial and personal information forms will be e-mailed to them. The potential client must fill out these forms and bring them to the initial consultation. The potential client is further told that bringing the completed forms to the meeting with an attorney will save time, so the focus of the consultation will be on providing legal advice and feedback and answering any and all of the potential client's questions.

---

1. There is an old sales adage that says the person asking the questions controls the conversation. That certainly applies here.

2. If the coordinator is not sure, the caller is informed that the coordinator will check with an attorney and call right back before setting an appointment. The time frame between ending the call, checking with an attorney, and calling back should be no more than one hour.

The potential client is then told that we charge a reduced rate of $200, for example, for this consultation and that it is payable in advance. If the potential client hesitates or asks why, the coordinator reiterates the value of the work the lawyer does reviewing the forms the client filled out and answering all of the client's questions. If necessary, the coordinator would also inform the client that the consultation has a value of more than $350 if charged at the regular rate. (If the caller asked why some firms give initial consultations for free, the coordinator responds, "That's because they are either personal injury firms that don't charge by the hour, or they may need to offer free consultations in order to get new business. This firm turns down more cases than it accepts. We are very selective of the cases and clients we accept. We don't need to give away our services."[3]

Result: Better Client Selection and Growth

Through years of experience, I determined that once the initial, in-office consultation was completed, both the attorney and the client had a much better chance of making a sound, informed decision about whether they wanted to do business together. Sophisticated clients appreciated the care and manner we used in collecting information and analyzing situations before committing to taking their case. They also were provided with a no-risk environment in which to assess who we were and how we do business.

None of my competitors provided as much of a detailed intake approach as my firm did. Although this type of approach might be considered a little laborious, I can assure you that the extra care up front before committing to a case or a client pays dividends on the back end when it comes to collecting fees for services provided. Because of this approach, my firm's steady growth compared to that of my competitors quickly became obvious. I was not only recouping a substantial share of lost billings by charging for in-office consultations, but I was eliminating the reduction in billable hours caused by the outdated practice of free telephone consultations. *We were answering and addressing every call that came into the firm, thereby converting a much*

3. Again, there is a little salesmanship here. We let the caller know that our firm is the one making the selection, not the other way around. This shifts the posture of the firm from seller to buyer.

larger percentage of phone calls into paying clients than those still clinging onto the old system.

As you are beginning to see, efficient information management leads to better client selection, which inevitably leads to fewer collection problems. It can also reduce the number of lost clients, thereby increasing the number of clients retaining your firm. If you don't want more clients, it will provide you the luxury of more choice about which clients to take. This will ultimately lead to better cash flow and increased profit. And this is the first essential piece of the puzzle of building a good ecosystem for practicing law.

Specific or Follow-Up Telephone Calls

In some situations a telephone call is not from a new caller but from a client, another attorney, or someone else. In this case, the coordinator acts more like the traditional receptionist, except that he or she uses the latest technology.

First, the coordinator should try to determine if the call relates to an ongoing case. If it does, the call should immediately be directed to the legal assistant (paralegal) in charge of the file. We haven't yet addressed this, but each file or case will be the responsibility of one legal assistant who is the go-to person for every communication or piece of information relating to that file or case. It is irrelevant whom the caller asks for. Most of the time, the legal assistant is available and more able to answer the caller's questions than even the responsible attorney. Most legal assistants are far more up to date on the status of cases, documents, or court proceedings than the attorney handling the cases. Being up to date should be a major part of the legal assistant's job description.

If the client, opposing counsel, or court personnel really wants to talk to the attorney directly after their concern or communication is handled by the legal assistant, the legal assistant can (1) transfer the call to the attorney if the attorney is available, (2) take a message, or (3) transfer the call to the attorney's voice mail. The reason behind this system is that most calls during the life of a case are status or information-seeking calls. If the attorney were to attempt to answer each call as it came in, he or she could be interrupted dozens of times each day. As a result, the attorney could lose massive amounts of productivity, momentum, and concentration on his or her priorities. In addition, the attorney would most likely refer the caller back to the legal assistant since the legal assistant can answer status-type questions such as whether someone was served, what the next court date is, or whether the firm received a given document. If you have one person in charge of the file (the physical file *in addition to* the entire status of the case itself), that person can operate efficiently and quickly to make sure everything is up to date and can communicate that information more effectively than anyone else in the office. Clients can be apprised of the many aspects of their cases by simply being copied on an e-mail or sent an e-mail with a scanned copy of a document received by or sent from your firm. This simple, ongoing practice will eliminate many status calls.

Finally, if messages are simply taken every time a call comes in for an attorney, and the attorney spends a substantial amount of time in court or in meetings, these messages begin to pile up, requiring more and more time to return. This practice is impractical and inefficient. It is far more efficient to have all these calls first handled by someone who is not only in a better position to handle them, but who can effectively reduce the number of interruptions or telephone messages piling up for the busy attorney.

Oh, and a note about telephone messages and those small pink telephone message forms or the ones in duplicate, three to a page. Forget that stuff! All messages should be transmitted by e-mail, and all e-mail should be kept and backed up. E-mail inboxes, sent mail folders, and e-mail folders named for individual clients can be sorted (by name, date, or keyword, for example) and searched within seconds to determine the status of a case or tasks assigned to or completed by staff in your firm. This method can eliminate tasks falling between the cracks or being overlooked under a mountain of other information bombarding the attorney or paralegal.

Years of e-mail can also be searched to determine if a person was called, a message given, or a document sent. And at least three computers will have this e-mail (the sender's computer, the receiver's computer, and the server) *in addition to* the backup media you have made from your server. This kind of system provides detailed and automatic record keeping, which takes up no physical space and is easily retrievable for a variety of purposes, not the least of which is billing. It comprises a large portion of automatic, responsible record keeping for your files while simultaneously serving as an efficient form of communication and information management.

Mail, Deliveries, E-mail, or Faxes

I once worked in a firm that had about seventy attorneys and their support staff spread over three floors of an office building. The time lag between the firm receiving a document (mailed or hand delivered) and the attorney being aware of the document could span two or three days or more! Attorneys who are in meetings or at court have higher priorities than checking everything as it comes in. The document often had to wait before anyone discovered it buried on the attorney's desk.

This was a very poor system. Here is a better one.

All documentation arriving at the office (or delivered to your department, if you have a larger firm) should be received and coordinated by one person—the intake coordinator. The duties of receiving and coordinating documents are not much different than those for handling the follow-up phone calls previously discussed. First, the coordinator should stamp the first page of all hard documentation with the date and time the document was received. Then it should be logged and scanned before being directed to the legal assistant responsible for the file or case. I don't think I need to explain why the stamping is so important. (If I do, then you've never argued over the date of service of documents, or the deadline date when discovery is due.)

The scanned document will automatically be attached to internal e-mails, either to the entire firm or to group e-mails, and be sent instantaneously to the proper personnel from the all-in-one copier/printer/scanner, which also serves as the network printer for a department or your entire firm, depending on its size. It is not the cute, desktop version sold at Costco, but the workhorse that you lease at great expense. The lease should include same-day servicing, and the machine should be able to feed documents at the rate of seventy pages per minute for copying or scanning. It is worth every penny.

For electronic service or delivery of documents, the firm should designate one email address only as its service email address. This email address can then be the responsibility of the intake coordinator. The coordinator will know to whom to send the documents because a chart that is updated weekly will be on the coordinator's desk or cork board, or it will be next to the central copier/printer/scanner. If the chart is near a desk, it should be in a binder to shield its contents from wandering eyes. This chart is updated every week at the case-review meetings (see Chapter 3). The chart indicates the firm clients down the left-hand column, and the personnel of the firm across the top row. The tasks to be accomplished by each member of the firm are in the box where each row and column meet. The legal assistant in charge of the file is also indicated at the top of the form next to the client or case name.

With this system, everyone involved with a particular file or case will receive almost instantaneously an internal e-mail message with a copy of the document attached and ready for printing or viewing. No unnecessary trees are cut down, and there's no delay in delivering a document that several people may want to get their hands on to review. And the firm has a clear record of what happened to the document after it arrived at the firm's door. Depending on the volume of documentation you are dealing with, you may instruct the coordinator to do this twice a day—once first thing in the morning to handle all late arrivals from the day before, and once after lunch or after the mail arrives each day. Anything that appears or is marked *urgent* or *important* can be delivered and e-mailed instantly by itself.

You should throw out your fax machine and have all faxes received by your intake coordinator's computer. Every fax will appear as just another e-mail, easily forwarded, printed, or filed. Since this type of system already converts a fax into a digital document (usually a PDF), it reduces extraneous paper handling. There's no need to receive a hard copy fax and convert it into a digital document. Faxing out can be done the same way in reverse if someone out there in Timbuktu, only has a fax machine and doesn't use e-mail. That is, you can e-mail a document, which pops out on that soon-to-be-anachronistic fax machine at the other end as a hard copy.

Just as I used to insist that the sun not set on unrecorded timekeeping (see Chapter 4), I also loathed the To Be Filed file on various administrative personnel desks. These To Be Filed files may be expandable accordion files or larger banker's boxes separated in alphabetical order by client name. You can imagine the serious problems that can develop with client Smith if each day the administrative assistant tries to catch up on the filing and starts with the letter *A* and only gets as far as *G* or *L* and starts up the next day or so, never getting to *S* for several days or weeks.

The solution to this is simple: you include updating the files daily as a part of that person's job description. This person is usually the legal assistant who is in charge of the file, or, for those legal assistants with larger caseloads or expanded duties, the assigned administrative assistant, who may be shared with another legal assistant. Whoever has the direct responsibility for filing hard copies or originals of documents needs to have in his or her daily calendar, with a pop-up reminder, to begin updating files a half hour or so before their expected departure from the office that day. *Every day.* This way, nothing is left to chance, and the assistant has to make a conscious effort to avoid meeting the responsibility, as opposed to an unconscious one.

2

HOW TO CHOOSE YOUR CLIENTS WELL

Initial Consultation

The first step in the client-selection process is the initial intake telephone call by the intake coordinator, which is also the most efficient method for answering and screening telephone calls as well as the initial step in moving the potential client to the first appointment. Critical portions of this step include (1) collecting information about the potential client, the case and related parties during the call, (2) sending and receiving forms that include more detailed personal and financial information about the client, (3) checking the forms for completeness and assisting the client in completing them before the initial consultation, and (4) collecting payment for the initial consultation.

The second step of the client selection process continues with the all-important initial consultation—the first face-to-face meeting between the lawyer and the potential client. Before this meeting takes place, here's what needs to be accomplished to complete the transition from first-time caller to potential client and, after the initial consultation, to firm client.

After the intake coordinator decides (or has an attorney help decide) that the caller may move to the next step, that of potential client, the coordinator e-mails financial forms and a background information form to the potential client. For family law cases in your jurisdiction, simply use the financial forms required to file divorce or dissolution pleadings. These forms typically include personal information such as names and ages of parties and children, date of marriage, and other relevant information for the court to understand the parameters of the case. For estate planning clients, provide a form requesting the relevant information needed to reveal the financial and family circumstances as a basis for developing a thoughtful and comprehensive estate plan. (If the potential client does not have a private e-mail or does not know how to use e-mail, then the intake coordinator mails the forms, and the client brings the filled-in forms to the initial consultation appointment.)

The intake coordinator places the completed financial and background information into a temporary file with the potential client's name on it. Also in the file is the intake form from the coordinator's phone interview. (Note: We use the traditional manila file folders for the temporary file. If and when the potential client becomes a firm client, the information gets transferred into the firm format of a client file. We use a three-ring binder, which we believe is eminently easier to navigate than a two-hole punch folder where extracting documents is a major hassle. The only exception is the exhibit file ultimately used for court, which is typically an expandable bucket-type folder (or banker's box for larger cases) with each exhibit inside in its own manila folder. The organization of these exhibits depends on how the information is used. Documents reflecting assets or debts can be organized in the same way as the court forms that summarize these items. For trials, documents can be organized in the order in which they will be presented at court.

The intake coordinator, who has already asked how the potential client will pay for the consultation, charges the credit card supplied during the intake phone call on the day of the initial consultation. Many times the client will simply bring in the filled-in forms and pay with cash or personal check on the day of the consultation. That is okay. But the preferred method is to have the payment complete and information received well before the day of the initial consultation. This accomplishes two important things. First, we find out that the potential client's credit card works, and we are assured of payment before providing the consultation. Second, the attorney has more time in which to review the information before sitting down with the potential client. Also, the intake coordinator has time to review the forms and call the potential client to fill in any blanks that the client missed or did not understand. Otherwise, when the client appears at the appointed time with the forms and payment, the intake coordinator checks the forms carefully to make sure the important information is filled in completely. If not, the coordinator works with the potential client immediately (in the privacy of the conference room) to fill in blanks on the forms.

There is a large variation in the way potential clients fill in the forms. Many do a precise job. Many others leave out birthdates, length of marriage, or real estate values—all critical information that impacts the attorney's ability to identify pertinent issues or potential complexities of the client's case. (If these gaps are not thoroughly addressed by the intake coordinator, the attorney wastes valuable time gathering basic information before beginning to give advice.) The intake coordinator also processes the payment for the initial consultation.

Strict adherence to this process is typically without exception. However, it can get out of hand if a view toward the big picture is missing. For example, a potential client forgot his checkbook when he appeared at our office for the initial consultation, and he apparently didn't have a credit card with him either. Before I ever saw him, he was rescheduled to the next week. At his second appearance, he again forgot to bring any means of payment (we were talking about $150.00) so the intake coordinator sent him to a nearby ATM to get the money. The potential client finally appeared an hour later (third time's the charm!) with the $150.00. Luckily, I was still available to conduct the initial consultation that day. Under both circumstances, the coordinator did the right thing. What she did not know was that the potential client's assets were many millions of dollars and he was in a thirty-year marriage. We easily could have lost this client to another law firm, but apparently the referral to our firm was so strong (more on this in Chapter 7) that the client put up with this inconvenience both times and persisted until he was finally "permitted" to meet with me. ("What's a fellow got to do to see a lawyer in this town?")

The case turned out to be the largest case of my career, both in total fees as well as in an attorney's fees award by the family court. Throughout six long years, I represented the client against five other law firms hired to represent the opposing party and ultimately the bank, who was refusing to release money to me that had been ordered by the court. I had actually settled the case within four months of its beginning, having gathered all the relevant financial information and made an offer of settlement to the opposing counsel. There were two of them. Upon acceptance of my settlement offer, both attorneys were summarily fired by the opposing party for, I think, accepting my settlement offer. Replacement counsel then spent the next five years attempting to rescind the acceptance of the settlement offer by both previous attorneys and block the unwinding of assets in the thirty-year marriage. The large attorney's fees award to my client reflected this bad-faith approach to marriage dissolution.

When the intake coordinator's job is complete, the potential client is asked to wait about ten minutes while the attorney reviews the information in preparation for the consultation. (This short delay is not necessary if the potential client has previously e-mailed the forms to your office.) By the way, don't ever let a potential client wait in the reception area for more than five minutes without informing them why he or she is waiting. Otherwise, the lawyer should, as soon as possible, walk out to the reception area, greet the potential client, introduce himself or herself, and escort the potential client into the conference room for the initial consultation.

No matter how small a law firm you have, a conference room should be a critical part of the office design. Some thrifty lawyers consider a conference room to be a luxury. I don't. First, the extra square footage is an infinitesimally small portion of your overhead compared to the wide variety of uses it provides, from depositions to firm-wide meetings to employee birthday parties. A conference room allows attorneys to design and decorate their individual workspace according to their individual tastes with little effect on clients or attorneys. The conference room becomes an indispensible place for firm members or guests to use for confidential communications, negotiations, depositions, or meetings of any sort.

Since the attorney has just reviewed the potential client's financial and personal background information, the attorney can discuss these matters with some familiarity with the potential client. The attorney's promptness and background knowledge will make a good first impression on the potential client.

It is worth mentioning that we attorneys no longer live in a world where people feel privileged to see us. Rather, we live in a world where there is steep competition within the profession and where long waits in the reception area reflect inefficiency, disrespect, and poor time management rather than the greater importance of the professional's time over that of the client. If the attorney has committed to memory the number or names of the potential client's children or length of marriage (or any one of a number of personal facts or statistics unique to the potential client), the potential client will get the impression that the attorney cared enough to have learned this information before their first meeting. I cannot impress upon you the importance of conveying subtle but clear impressions to potential clients that you are organized, that you care about their case, and that you are not overselling the results you can deliver.

The most common mistake an attorney can make—a mistake that has the most devastating effect on long-term success—is to oversell or overpromise the results he or she can deliver in a given case. The fact of the matter is that the attorney only knows what the potential client has said in one meeting. These facts have not been verified, and the other side of the story has not been received. Hence, any overpromise of positive results only sets up future disappointment in a client from whom fee collection will be more difficult, and from whom unending amounts of negative feedback may be spewed among that client's peers and friends.

Clients only remember what you promised. They do not remember your caveats or how they may have inaccurately communicated the information about their case. And, even though clients have been informed (in your retainer agreement or personally by you) that you are paid for your time and not for results, setting up high expectations only invites disappointment in eventual results.

Again, the strength of the referral is almost as important as the initial consultation when it comes to the potential client's decision-making process. I once interviewed a famous local musician whom I did not recognize (he was known mostly by his first name). When I asked him about his line of business, I finally realized to whom I was talking. It wasn't a great first impression. However, I asked him how he was referred to our firm and he said, "I asked a friend who he used for his divorce, and my friend said, 'Forget my lawyer; my lawyer got his a-- kicked by Frank Lockwood. Call him!'" In that case, the fact that I did not recognize this local celebrity was not going to stop this client from hiring our firm. He was sold before coming into our office. The only question he came in to get answered was whether he could meet our retainer requirement.

Early in my career, I used a checklist of every possible issue in a divorce case as a guide in my initial consultations. I placed it in front of me to make sure I covered everything. After several years of using the checklist faithfully, I no longer needed it, but my staff always provided one in the temporary file as a backup. I strongly suggest that attorneys who have practiced in an area for less than five years use a checklist, which is also useful for new attorney training. After I stopped using this checklist, I usually made a quick list on my yellow pad (before the consultation began) of all potential issues identified by the intake coordinator or by my review of the financial or other information. I always reviewed this list before I ended the consultation to insure that we covered everything.

I start out every initial consultation by informing the client that the meeting is just an information and feedback session—that the client has not yet hired our firm to represent him or her and that I will not be giving the client advice to do anything that affects the case until we have a signed contract to handle their particular matter. I do inform the client that everything he or she says in this meeting is protected by the attorney-client privilege. (In the cases where a client brings along a friend or relative, I inform the client that this privilege does not extend to the other person ie., potentially, the friend or relative can be compelled at some later date to reveal facts or advice given at the meeting.) I also inform the client that once this meeting is over, neither the client nor the firm has an obligation to continue any kind of relationship. I also inform the client that at the end of the meeting I may present him or her with a retainer agreement to take home, read carefully, and consider signing. I will also, to the extent I am able, set a retainer amount for their case. I explain that the word *retainer* means "a deposit against future fees and costs incurred in the case."

I then inform the client that I will identify and discuss potential issues I see from the information he or she has provided us. However, I would prefer to start out with knowing what the potential client's foremost concerns are. This way, I get him or her talking, and I am able to better evaluate what kind of person I am dealing with. After all, issues of abuse or custody or potential fraud do not surface easily on these forms. (By the way, the intake coordinator also has asked this same question during the intake call. My experience is that only about fifty percent of potential clients reveal sensitive information or issues over the phone to a stranger.) So it merits asking the same question again in person, behind closed doors where the potential client feels safer.

Most attorneys are better talkers than listeners. And despite the fact that the attorney may want to impress the potential client in the hopes that he or she may be retained, the more important function of the initial consultation is to gather both relevant information and ancillary information (including the attorney's impressions of the client and his or her motivations) to make an informed decision about whether this client and case are appropriate for the firm. Listening also demonstrates that you care about what *the client* thinks is important even more than all the knowledge or legal jargon that might emerge from your mouth.

I provide potential clients candid and conservative feedback on their cases. That is, I do not provide the assurances about possible outcomes. (I do provide a range-of-outcomes assessment, if asked.) I also inform a potential client what the law is and how it might apply to his or her factual circumstances based upon what the potential client is telling me. I also inform the potential client that many times the court is presented with contradictory or conflicting factual information or testimony by an opposing party and will have to make a determination of which information it will use in making a decision.

I am acutely aware that many times the potential client will color or spin information to make the case appear more meritorious than it really is. (I know this is hard to believe.) That is relatively easy to deal with. Each time the potential client asserts an opinion or factual statement that is somewhat biased or strongly in their favor, I ask, "How would your spouse (or opposing party) respond to this?" Many clients are surprisingly candid with their answers to this question, and I am frequently shocked at some of the answers. Often the real "truth" is found in that answer or somewhere in between.

One time a female client in a custody case responded to this question by saying, "He'll say I'm an alcoholic." I asked, gently, "Do you have any drinking challenges that you can identify?" "Of course not!" she asserted, "I'm just a social drinker." I informed her that the easiest way to dispense with that potential red herring was to get an alcohol assessment done from a professional. I later withdrew from this case a few months later when the client failed, for the third consecutive time, to appear at her appointment for this assessment. Each failure was accompanied by an increasingly feeble excuse and a lie I caught her in. After I terminated our relationship, I was contacted by her father (who had provided the retainer and signed the retainer agreement as guarantor of fees) to discuss the return of the remaining retainer. In that conversation, I also found out that she had borrowed $10,000 from her father for a retainer, and given me only $5,000.00!

So asking about the opposing party's position can be a very valuable case-assessment tool. I usually ask the client to reconcile such different perspectives. This is also a valuable discussion to have. It frequently will smoke out clients who are exaggerating or even lying about their cases. There is nothing more suspicious than a client who portrays him- or herself as a complete, consistent angel in a marriage of twenty-five years while being married to a devil. As a formidable colleague of mine used to say, "They travel in pairs." This perspective has been confirmed time and again. Three of my most highly conflicted divorce cases have resulted in the clients reconciling *after* the divorce. In my mind, this nullifies basically every nasty thing they said publicly or privately about their spouse. Very confounding, especially after you have given your time, emotions, and worry to such clients.

As I am discussing each and every issue in the potential client's case, I take notes, numbering and naming each issue on my yellow pad. I also include a summary of the facts collected and advice given. If I am unable to write down everything that was discussed during the meeting, I complete my notes immediately after the meeting when the discussion is still fresh in my mind.

Once the substantive part of our discussion is complete, or we have gone over an hour and a half, I proceed to the business part of our potential relationship and explain how our firm does business. It is critical that the client understand how your firm administratively processes a client's case. It is equally important to use this information when a client tries to negotiate the terms of your relationship differently than is your custom.

I review the retainer agreement, pointing out and explaining the most important provisions. I further explain that the retainer agreement provides that once our fee is earned and the money transferred from the client's trust account into our business account, the client agrees to replenish the amount transferred from the trust account in order to restore it to its original balance.[1] I even draw a diagram on my yellow pad explaining how the money flows from the client to the client's trust account and then, after billing, the money is transferred from the client's trust account into the firm's business account. I then use the diagram to show that the client replenishes the client's trust account by the amount billed. This process is also explained in the retainer agreement, but I find that a graphic is helpful and clearly informs the potential client how our system works and what his or her obligations are.

Most small law firms don't use this system to make sure fees are paid promptly and retainer money is always available for their work. In fact, they wait until they are out of money, and discover that they have worked way beyond the client's immediate ability to pay. Sound familiar? There are two basic reasons why this occurs:

1. The attorney/owner has not assigned someone to keep an eye on all trust account balances and inform the owner on a periodic basis when there are problems.
2. It usually takes the firm four to six weeks to generate invoices for services performed, so that the firm is unaware for this period of time whether the client has run out of funds.

These are two of the chief causes of all accounts receivable challenges in small law firms. The solution to this problem is the system described in Chapter 4.

I conclude the meeting by providing the potential client with a copy of the firm's retainer agreement that has the initial retainer amount included. I tell the client to go home and think seriously before signing the agreement and paying the retainer. Not closing the deal when the client is in the room is a poor strategy for a car salesman, but I feel it is far more important to let the client—and you—simmer and reflect before making this commitment. The last time I made an exception to this procedure and others (like getting a parent to sign as guarantor), the client had big blue eyes, told a preposterous

1. We titled ours Legal Representation Agreement rather than retainer because, despite explanations, most folks still struggle with the term "retainer."

story, and eventually filed Chapter 7 bankruptcy, thereby avoiding paying the $150,000 in fees I had earned. The good news is that, because I had otherwise stayed true to the system that year and thereafter, I hardly felt the difference financially. How many other small law firms can say that? In my case, the hurt was only emotional.

After the client leaves, I turn to my computer (or dictation system) and draft an e-mail summarizing the case, the client, my impressions, and any conditions, if applicable, that need to be met before accepting this client and case. This e-mail goes to the office manager and intake coordinator, with a hard copy placed in the temporary file until the potential client returns the retainer agreement along with the specified retainer. But let's not get ahead of ourselves. One of the most important aspects of a successful practice is client selection. Let's examine that.

Client Selection Process

Your Behavior

The client becomes a combination of the person who appears at your office and the person who leaves after interacting with you. He or she is typically a changed person because of your interaction with them. The question is *Is the client better or worse as a result of that experience?* The answer depends in large part on how you handled your initial consultation. If you are desperate for work, desperate for cash flow, or a little too reckless with your opinions, the client will emerge from your office as damaged goods. And if you take him or her on as a client, you will pay for it.

The purpose of these caveats is to warn attorneys not to oversell the case presented to them, and not to promise excellent results. As indicated above, it is irresponsible to promise anything since you have just heard no more than half the case. And you have just set the client up with higher expectations than may be warranted under the circumstances. The chances of meeting these illusionary expectations are minimal. Hence, you have just created a future, unhappy client who may resist paying your bill.

I know you want to appear confident and knowledgeable to the potential client. But don't let this desire spill over to acting invulnerable—or worse, appearing like you are the client's white knight—in an attempt to influence their hiring decision. Once again, you will have created a monster that later you will have to battle for fees. Why go through it all? The more prudent, long-term approach is to be conservative with your opinion regarding outcome projections and assure the client that you will do your best to achieve maximum results. If that is not good enough for the potential client (for example, if the client argues with you about what the potential results should be, or worse, presses you for guarantees), do not take him or her on as a client. You are only headed for trouble if you do.

I realize that I have repeated this point many times. It is the attorney who sets the expectation level of the client. If the client refuses to have his or her expectations lowered or is disappointed in your opinions, don't take the client. It is better to part ways immediately rather than after the relationship becomes messy and you lose more billable time.

Your Standards

As I've stated in many seminars, if you take on that case only because the client has the retainer you need to meet this month's overhead, you have entered a vicious, negative cash-flow cycle. Operating this way may take months to cure and involve a credit line from the bank until you can get your finances in order. I know; I've been there. In addition, I watched as an of counsel in my office created an accounts receivable balance twice the size of her revenue in just one year. I severed the relationship immediately before it cost me more money than she was bringing in. For my part, I made the mistake of not contractually requiring her to adhere to my system of billing and collection. She had no system of her own. So if you're doing any kind of office sharing or of counsel arrangement, make sure that the attorney is staying on top of the billing and collection, or better yet, that you are responsible for keeping this part of the attorney's system operating efficiently. More on this in Chapter 4.

We have already spoken about charging for the initial consultation. That in itself will disqualify a huge portion of potential clients who do not value, or cannot pay for, your services. So if you think you have lost a potential client because he or she refused to pay for the initial consultation, you have only lost a potential headache. It's better to go home early and spend time with your family rather than to work on a case for which you will never get paid.

Red flags that may signal clients who will prove to be problematic are a lack of reasonableness and flexibility and an inability to look at the case from the opponent's point of view. Potential clients who refuse to acknowledge any redeeming value in the opposing party or its merits will similarly make an enemy out of you by the end of the case. These clients are damaged goods coming into your office. Sometimes you can fix them. Most of the time you cannot.

Ability to Pay

It is not only permissible to ask a potential client how they intend to pay your fees—it is critical. You want to know that the client has thought about this before he or she even called your office. And you want to hear what the client has to say. Many times the answer will lead to the signature of a guarantor who is a parent or other relative. Other times, if the client has underestimated the potential fees in the case, you may be able to assist them in brainstorming additional sources of payment. If there is no way to determine how the client is going to pay your entire fees, you can explore seeking payment from the opposing party. This is a definite risk that you alone will incur. If you can only assess, for example, that half of your fees may be paid from assets or credit, then you must realistically acknowledge that you may take a fifty percent discount on this case. Don't be surprised several months down the road if the client suddenly is unable to pay the balance owed to you. The client always had that inability. You just didn't notice it.

Some firms take on cases they know the client cannot pay for, especially if the case proceeds to discovery and litigation. These firms keep track of the client's available funds, and once these funds run out, the firm moves to withdraw from representing the client. I think this approach is potentially unethical, especially if the firm made this calculation as part of their cash flow system well in advance of the withdrawal. Most states require a judge's approval of this withdrawal. I wish the judge would ask if upon retention the law firm had any inkling that the client could not pay the full fare. If the attorney admits that he or she knew this was a distinct possibility, the court should make the firm eat the rest of the case and deny the motion to withdraw.

None of these analyses are easy questions. In fact, they can be quite complicated and lean on the side of negative. But it is worth it to take your time to make these analyses, even if it means losing a few potential billable hours. It may save you dozens of unpaid hours later on. An ounce of prevention....

Client's Reasonableness

If the client's goals in or assessment of the case do not line up with yours, do not take the case. Again, you will only have an unhappy client at the end who will refuse to pay your bill (even if you told the client so in a beautifully written disclaimer letter). Why go through the agony?

When you are finished analyzing the case, you are ready to accept it if (1) the potential client and you determine the case has merit, (2) the potential client is reasonable, and (3) the potential client can pay your fees.

It is that simple. Almost.

One additional caveat: Every time you ignore your gut, you usually pay for it. If it helps, bring in an associate or legal assistant who is skilled at discerning people to assist you. Or after the consultation, go consult with one of these folks in your office and be open to honest feedback.

Once this system became part of our standard procedures, in addition to the firm making more money, life in the office improved overall, and I began to look forward to representing clients who were responsible enough to meet their obligations. Of course, this is not the end of the story. The client-selection process continued to evolve to the point that we began looking at several additional factors before deciding to take on a case. Cases that were too small and hence not cost effective were referred to newer attorneys building their practices. We began sculpting the firm's reputation in handling cases involving complex business and real estate valuations, for example. These additional factors, together with the basics indicated above, allowed us to steer the firm in the direction we wanted to go. Instead of desperately hoping more clients would hire me, I changed to cautiously deciding which potential clients fit within the parameters of the direction we wanted the firm to pursue.

There remains only one step to the potential client making the transition to becoming a full-fledged firm client: the retainer agreement.

Retainer Agreements

The hallmark of any good law practice is a thorough and comprehensive retainer agreement. Because the word *retainer* rarely has meaning to the average client, I referred to my retainer agreement as a Legal Representation Agreement, or LRA, because that's exactly what it was—my agreement to represent a client for a particular matter, in consideration of the client paying me according to the various terms listed in the agreement. Many attorneys argue for a simple one- or two-page agreement, so that the client can more easily understand it.

I don't.

In fact, my LRA expanded and became more detailed over the years as it became time- and court-tested. I created additional provisions that could save me time and money and could make enforcement and collection much easier. Each time I sought to add a provision to my LRA, I would run it by ethics counsel in my state to make sure I wasn't running afoul of any guidelines. I advise you to do this as well. In fact, should you adopt my sample LRA, I would run the entire agreement past your ethics counsel to make sure it complies with your jurisdiction's particular guidelines.[2]

Whether you adopt part or all of my sample LRA, a comprehensive LRA should contain the following information or provisions:

1. Client's contact information, including Social Security number
2. The particular matter for which the firms is being hired
3. A list of obligations agreed to by the client
4. A list of duties to be performed by the firm, both in general and specific terms
5. A list of exceptions of duties or tasks that are *not* covered by the LRA
6. A payment section that lists the hourly rates of personnel that may work on client's case, as well as a list of particular reimbursable expenses incurred by the firm on behalf of the client. It should also include specific due dates for invoices, interest rates for overdue payments, and lien language on any settlements due the client. This particular lien language is ethically required in many states, and it is invaluable since it

2. A copy of a sample Legal Representation Agreement is attached as Appendix 2.

may serve to avoid additional court work and act as escrow instructions by former clients who forgot the value of services you provided just a few months ago.

7. A paragraph explaining, in detail, how the system of advance payments, sometimes referred to as retainers, works, including your withdrawal of these payments from the client's trust account into your firm's business account, and the client's obligation to reimburse the trust account within a specified time period.
8. A list of reasons that authorize your firm to withdraw from representation.
9. Statements that the results are not guaranteed and that the client has read and understood the agreement. Personnel in the firm are required to make sure that the last item is handled with care and consistency when a client first hires the firm. Prospective clients are instructed to go home and read the LRA carefully and completely before signing, and urged to ask questions about any provisions they don't understand before signing it. Notes of these instructions should be included in the notes of every initial consultation. You would be surprised that because of these provisions a large number of collection cases against clients who claimed never to have read the LRA before signing were successful.
10. The final, and arguably the most important, section is the client information section, which includes such provisions as driver's license number, two credit card numbers, and the same information for guarantors of the agreement. All these provisions have been tested and used successfully to collect fees owed by clients. Invoking their use requires judgment as to whether their use will result in a disciplinary complaint or lawsuit. Discretion is recommended.

3

HOW TO IMPLEMENT A FAIL SAFE CASE MANAGEMENT SYSTEM

Introduction

In most areas of our lives, those of us with controlling natures wonder whether (and when) we need to back off and let nature take its course. In areas of love, child rearing, and family activities, we can't always be (and don't want to be) in charge. So what about the organization and direction of our case flow and management? Well, the answer is very simple: *Totally control it, or it will control you*. There is no gray area here.

Most attorneys abhor what they call "admin" work. Of course, they are referring to the business side of law practice that they think has little, if anything, to do with being a lawyer. Some even consider it demeaning. Regardless of the perspective, administrative work is usually relegated to the bottom of the pile for case or administrative staff, and attorneys get to it only when they can fit it in. Or administrative work is addressed when attorneys are forced to deal with circumstances demanding their immediate attention. Or worse, when they are confronted by frustrated administrative employees who are trying to do their jobs properly and are stymied by a process—for example, you, the owner, want to do things the ways they've always been done. Many times it is you, the owner, who becomes the roadblock or bottleneck of efficient firm administrative systems. The predictable results of this type of behavior are stress, unhappy employees, chronic emergencies, poor cash flow, and lower profits. Yet few small firm attorneys can see above the pile of work on their desk to find a better way. There is a better way and it is described in detail in this book.

All you need is the information in this book and the discipline (or personnel) to implement it. Once you do, your personal and professional life will change for the better forever. Did you think you could keep your head in the rarified air of your law practice while the rest of your non-lawyer staff cleaned up your messes? You already know the answer to that question.

The entire focus of this book, if you haven't figured it out by now, is to embrace and systematize (rather than avoid) the administrative processes of running a small law firm. The "magic" if you will, is to set up administrative processes once and for all and stick to them. Religiously. What most small firm lawyers do is avoid them and end up repeating portions of these processes over and over again, and only when forced to do so. Then they wonder why they spend their lives putting out fires that could have been avoided with proper planning and systems in place. Once the systems are put into place, the boring admin work, although repeated week after week, is minimal, rote, and actually freeing. No matter how boring it may seem, when applied to case management, for example, boring is actually what you're trying to achieve. (It is something like golf. An exciting round of golf is usually a bad round. A round of golf with no surprises is usually a brilliant round. Ask any golfer.)

The results of sound case management, however, are anything but boring. They simply lack drama, which is what you want. Results such as case success, smoother cash flow, less stress, increased profits, and happier clients are well worth it. Aren't these the types of hard-to-define goals we want to achieve, after all?

Finally, it is important to know that sticking to these systems is not something I love to do. It's more like flossing your teeth. You only need to floss the ones you want to keep. So I keep doing it despite the short-term irritation and basic dislike of the process. (I floss my teeth every night as well.) The long-term benefits are worth it.

I stress this because I think it is important to know that I am the last person whose personality lends itself to this type of systems thinking. I love shooting from the hip, thinking out loud, and all the other spontaneous types of behavior that (I find) are so entertaining and valuable at parties and seminars and in the courtroom, given proper preparation. However, despite what I may think are my talents and personality traits, I think we can all agree that proper planning trumps just about all those other skills and traits. I lost many cases in my early years to boring, methodical lawyers who had out-prepared me. It soon became clear that thorough preparation, both in a case and in the office, held the secrets to success.

What follows is a relatively simple and straightforward system I developed so that I was certain I knew all that was happening in my cases and with my clients well ahead of the time when I needed to prepare something or react to opposing counsel.

Remember the TV series *LA Law*? I actually remember the very first episode. In it, an attractive female client provides Arnie Becker, the firm's family lawyer, with a settlement agreement. She says, "My husband and I are in agreement on everything. I don't want to fight. Please look this over just in case there are some problems I do not see." (Or something like that.)

Instead of studying the document, Arnie scuttles the settlement by hiring a photographer to take photos of the husband in compromising positions with his previously unknown girlfriend. Arnie then invites his client (the wife) to lunch in a nice restaurant and casually hands her the photos as they are preparing to order. She looks at the photos and totally freaks out. Now she wants to fight! (It turns out that her husband was hiding assets, which Arnie later discovered. But how did he know that?) I thought, *OMG, is this what my mother thinks I do for a living?*

Weekly Case-Review Meetings

More to the point, each episode of *LA Law* began with the attorneys meeting around the conference table, discussing the status of cases with trials or depositions scheduled for that day, the challenges needing to be met for those cases, and the resources that could be applied or reallocated to meet those challenges. I believe the television writers wanted a convenient way to introduce the various plots of each week's episode. In theory, this is not a bad idea, but in practice, it is way too late, as any of us practitioners know, to decide what is needed in a case on the very day it's needed.

Because of their ever-changing nature and priority status, cases need to be discussed, and tasks defined and assigned, sometimes weeks or months in advance, and then reviewed over and over again. This is a total pain. (Remember flossing?) Most lawyers have trouble getting past the next task in a case, and too often, most tasks are in reality a response to some action initiated by the other party. Worse yet, most practitioners don't even have case-review meetings on any kind of periodic basis. They schedule them only when there is an emergency or a time-sensitive deadline created by the court or the opposing party. Most of the time, it's too late to have any beneficial effect except for maybe avoiding malpractice. Perhaps it's not necessarily too late to meet a court or discovery deadline, but it's usually too late to avoid the stress of piling that deadline upon other cases or tasks, already imminent, or with already stressed resources. So, is there a better way? Of course there is.

This begs the question: *When is the best time to schedule a case review or case status meeting?* The answer is very simple: when it's *not* needed. Huh? Yes, that's right. We scheduled weekly case review meetings every Friday morning. (This day was chosen because the family court in our jurisdiction held no hearings on Fridays, so that there were few conflicts with court dates. It also provided us with a jump on the next week before the weekend.)

We reviewed the cases in alphabetical order, including where we were in each case and where we wanted to go, and what challenges and resources we needed to address on cases with deadlines that were approaching in the next few weeks. New cases took more time because we used this time to plot out the entire potential timeline and case strategy and put it on its own computerized calendar, complete with advance reminders of looming deadlines. Larger, more complicated cases would have their own scheduled case review, perhaps monthly, to plan and schedule out the work and needed resources (money, personnel), and to have the timing and deadlines calendared.

Estimates were also made of the hours needed to perform the tasks laid out. (These estimates of hours for attorneys and legal assistants were frequently revised as the nature of the case changed, or as additional unanticipated demands were put on the case by opposing parties.)

Case Tracking

Two forms were used for these purposes. One was a detailed multi-page form for each case, which included every possible task that might need to be performed, who was responsible to perform it, and a blank space for the date performed and the person performing it. The other form was also a multi-page, less detailed form, which included all the active cases handled by the firm. In columnar form, it included the name of the client, the legal assistant responsible for the file, the attorney(s) responsible for the case, and a summary of the case status. Discussions alternated from free-flowing brainstorming to repeated, ordered reviews of the detailed chronology of each case.

The meetings were attended by every attorney and legal assistant in the firm—whether they were involved in any given case or not. The only exception to this rule involved attorneys or legal assistants who were working on imminent deadlines for their cases. However, these exceptions were rare. The default was that everyone was required to attend these meetings. (Note: in larger firms with different departments, this system may be adapted to specific departments rather than the entire firm.)

We structured case-tracking meetings this way for two major reasons. First, the unstructured input of those not directly involved in a case frequently resulted in a fresh perspective and new ideas. Second, the process acted as a training session for younger attorneys and legal assistance to improve their skills and perspectives and build experience. If you've ever watched the television series *House* you'll see how brainstorming diagnostics of a disease is a discovery, free-thinking, planning, and training session all rolled into one. Our meetings served much the same function. (I was not as obnoxious or condescending as Dr. House was, however.)

The meetings were not attended by administrative staff. However, the accounts receivable, billing person in the firm who also doubled as my office manager and human resources department was provided with the written results of this meeting. That person met with me weekly to review the status of the client trust account balances. We compared these balances to the work that needed to be done to determine if the accounts receivable billing person needed to communicate with the client regarding payment of additional retainers and the reasons (as indicated in the list of tasks in their case). More on that in Chapter 5.

File Organization and Responsibility

Each case—its file organization and its planning—was assigned to a paralegal, not a lawyer. Why? Because I found that paralegals usually had better organizational skills than attorneys. They were able to stay ahead of the work needing to be done (the procedural aspects of the case), while having a moderate understanding of the substantive aspects of the case. Another way of putting this, the paralegal's primary concern was procedural, while his or her understanding of the substantive aspects of the case was shallower. The attorney's focus was just the opposite. The attorney could focus on deep, substantive thinking and preparation without worrying about deadlines. This seemed to be a complementary marriage of skills.

4

HOW TO IMPLEMENT AN INTEGRATED TIMEKEEPING, BILLING, AND COLLECTION SYSTEM

One of the two areas where lawyers frequently fall short is implementing an integrated timekeeping, billing, and collection system. As a result, they often wonder why they experience cash flow challenges and ever-increasing accounts receivable. (The other area is choosing the right clients, discussed in Chapter 2.)

Many law firms, small and large, become overly dependent on bank lines of credit, which, while a sound practice when used as a fallback, are problematic when they become part of a regular monthly cash-flow system. Thousands of dollars get flushed down the toilet in the form of needless interest payments each year. Instead, that money could have been spent on a new BMW lease (or monthly contributions to a retirement fund). This poor trade-off is the result of poor discipline and lack of systems. We will discuss how to wean yourself off of the line-of-credit vicious cycle, or at least, how to minimize the fees paid when you must use it (see Chapter 9).

Photos on Your Desk

Before I became an attorney, I always wondered why busy executives with nice offices kept family photos on their desk or credenza. I figured it was just a part of the checklist when you became part of the establishment. Country club membership, check; Rotary Club, check; family photos on the desk, check.

Then, one day after I had been practicing on my own for a few years, I was upset at the umpteenth client who now could not seem to pay for my services. It was then that a realization changed my entire perspective as a professional. Until this time, I had felt privileged to have a law degree (despite my blue-collar roots and, further, despite the fact that I still owed thousands of dollars on law school loans), and I felt somewhat guilty for the poor souls who needed my legal services but could not afford to pay for them. (I'm not talking about a commitment to do pro bono work, which I believe in, and will discuss later.) I am referring to the lack of a conscious business system for *client selection* and *case management* where pro bono work is a choice, not an unintended result.

I happened to glance at the photo of my wife and daughters on my desk and realized that I had just given hours of my time away to someone who was a stranger just a few weeks ago. All of a sudden, it occurred to me that if I was going to spend time for which I would not be paid, I would much rather spend that time with my family than with some random stranger who just happened to find me in the yellow pages. It was then and there that I made a commitment that I would not consciously give my time away again.

But how was I going to change my procedures to prevent this from happening again? I instituted two simple procedures:

1. I decided that if a client determined, sometime in the midst of the case, that he or she did not have the money to pay for continued services, I would consider withdrawing from representation of the client. Yes, until this time I felt it was my moral obligation to finish the case, regardless

of the client's ability to pay—or actually, change in values about paying—for my services. Perhaps it was something my parents taught me. Finish your dinner. Finish your chores. Finish the case?

2. After withdrawal, I would institute a collection action (through outside counsel) against those clients who were gainfully employed and for whom I could get a judgment and garnishee their wages. In our jurisdiction, it was also possible to become a creditor in the very case from which you were withdrawing, and receive an order establishing payment of your fee balance once proceeds were distributed in that case.

These decisions turned out to be the framework, albeit skeletal, of an integrated billing-and-collection system.

Within six months of making this decision, something strange happened. My net income, which was not much in those days, doubled. Yes, doubled. I was ecstatic and so was my wife. She was also glad that she did not have to listen to me moan at dinner about another client not paying me and about my ever-increasing accounts receivable. I was not working any harder. What I was doing, in essence, was working only for those clients that were paying me. What a concept!

My point? In many ways, mostly unconscious and often traditional, lawyers by default do things that they had no intention of doing. But since we have no conscious system of prevention in place, we begin heading down a path of nonproductive, unintentional pro bono work. We are, in effect, letting the randomness of our clients determine when our work would be pro bono. Perhaps we feel a little guilty because of the hourly rate we charge compared to the hourly rate clients receive from their jobs. Who knows? In any event, you can clearly see why cash flow challenges occur when your accounts receivable "system" is a random occurrence determined by random clients. This sounds odd, but it is what most small firm lawyers do. And worse, because of habit or tradition, this random system becomes imbedded as part of the firm's procedures with a momentum that is difficult (but not impossible) to change. Let's just say, to paraphrase Isaac Newton, "An object in motion tends to stay in motion." A bad system tends to continue unabated until a conscious decision is made to change it and implementation of the new system is accomplished.

Once I decided to stop representing clients who could not pay me and collect from former clients who could, the basic structure of an integrated system was born. In the years to come, I simply kept identifying consequences of other unconscious actions or gaps in my system that needed filling, and I implemented a solution as part of what was to become an effective system for reducing accounts receivable and increasing profit. What follows are discrete parts of that system. Each time members of your firm master any one of these parts, your firm's profit will increase. Each time someone in your firm drops the ball on, or deviates from, one of these parts, your profit will decrease. It's that simple.

Timekeeping Chaos

I have a cousin who is a partner in a large law firm with thousands of lawyers in offices all over the world. We recently discussed some of his firm's procedures and his personal challenges with turning in his timesheets in a timely manner. Basically, the firm deducts $100 from his partnership draw every time he is late turning in his timesheets. The firm gives him three days to turn in his timesheets and actually allows three missed deadlines per month before this $100 fine is assessed. Then, if he misses another three-day deadline, he is fined $100. Some partners in the firm lose thousands of dollars each year as a result of this practice. For those that make upwards of $300,000 to $500,000 per year, this is hardly an effective incentive to turn your timesheets in on time. It's like Michael Jordan getting fined $10,000 when he made upwards of $50,000 per game. Big deal.

The other problem with this approach is that it tries to solve a problem from the back end. It does not get at the root of the problem: i.e., the lack of a timekeeping system that works for each billable attorney and in which billing is done contemporaneously with the work. It amazes me that a firm whose sole revenue is the result of timekeeping and billing does not spend more effort or money to resolve this somewhat obvious, and apparently systemic, challenge with its own attorneys.

It's like giving the keys to your car to your teenager who has no driver's training and then expecting the teen to learn driving skills through the state-imposed rules and regulations for stopping, speeding, and so on. Finally (sorry, Cousin), setting the deadline at three days for turning in timesheets (after three free passes) only exacerbates the problem. In effect, the attorney is allowed three full days to forget as much of his work as possible before being forced to attempt to recollect what he or she actually did.

Doesn't it make more sense to require timesheets to be turned in early the next day so that only one night separates the attorney from the work that must be must recollected and recorded? Even then, recollecting which client you did what for and for how long on the previous day can be challenging. I'd hate to be the attorney cross-examined about the absolute accuracy of this method of timekeeping. My cousin says the firm simply expects its attorneys to figure out how to keep time since, hey, they work for a prestigious firm.

Really?

Timekeeping Solutions

Background

I spent three years in a large firm in Honolulu and noticed a large variation in the billable hours among lawyers in the firm. The firm published the monthly billable hours to every attorney, I guess, as a way to produce competition among them. This had little or no effect, since typically the same attorneys consistently billed about the same hours each month. There seemed to be a pattern that the same attorneys who produced high billable hours did it consistently, and the others consistently produced average or low billable hours per month. This intrigued me. So I set out to find out why.

I discovered a wide array of methods or techniques that each of these attorneys employed or simply copied from other attorneys, and these methods produced an equally wide array of results. There was no firm-wide method of timekeeping at all—no investigation into the worst or best methods, no advocacy or training within the firm devoted to making their attorneys more effective timekeepers. This huge disparity between the importance of timekeeping and any training to improve it still persists in most firms today.

Personally, I had experienced the same challenges when tracking my time that many of the attorneys I surveyed had experienced, from going to lunch and realizing I had one billable hour recorded while I had been in the office working hard for three or four hours, to arriving in the office in the morning and being able to recall only four hours of billable time from the previous day when I been there nine or ten hours.

Does any of this sound familiar?

Here's what I did. I interviewed dozens of attorneys and legal assistants who freely shared their methods and challenges in timekeeping. What I discovered is that there were many tricks and systems out there, each more or less adaptable to attorneys, depending on the individual attorney's skill set and discipline. I also learned that there was a lot of "fudging" going on, whereby attorneys were simply estimating time spent to fill out a day's work. That is, attorneys would acknowledge that they worked, say, eight hours that day and that they had spent about equal time on each of four clients' cases. As a result, they logged two hours per client for that day. (*Fudging* may be a euphemism.) I then experimented with many (not all) of the tips and techniques I had learned from these interviews. Some worked for me, others not so much. My timekeeping improved by about ten percent once I settled on a few techniques that I trained myself to follow. As you will see, that ten percent can be the difference in breaking even or making a healthy profit in your business—not because of an increase in business, but because of an increase in skill or discipline in using a system that works for doing basically the same amount of work.

When I started my own firm, I simply discussed the variety of methods with each new attorney or legal assistant, and encouraged them to experiment with any or a combination of methods. If their results were less than optimal, I worked with them one-on-one to try new methods or a combination of methods to improve their results. This proved effective every time except with one attorney and a few legal assistants. Month after month, the attorney continued to record about fifty percent of what he should have been recording, and he finally became frustrated at my frequent attention to his inability to record all of his time. He resigned apparently knowing that there were few options left.

Two of the legal assistants simply resorted to cheating on their time and were fired. Apparently they figured that I would not notice large blocks of time devoted to certain clients that produced few, or worse, poor, results. Did they think that I would not be reviewing their timesheets and work?

I also held in-house seminars on the subject every year to share the most effective systems used in the firm. Sometimes legal assistants or lawyers would develop new systems that they never got around to sharing. Some of these techniques used software that had been improved over the previous year. These new techniques would come up during the annual seminar and benefit many of us. Sometimes the seminar was just brushing up on our timekeeping skills.

The main point of all this is pretty simple. Like every other system in this book, I did not leave this critical aspect of running a law firm to chance. I made sure that this area of the practice was performed as consciously as possible with some form of consistency and regularity among the timekeepers.

Timekeeping Techniques and Policies: Ten Best Practices

Here are some of the timekeeping techniques and policies that should become part of your firm's written policies:

1. I required that all timesheets, in whatever form, were turned in by 10 a.m. the following morning for the previous day. This policy, in and of itself, accomplished nothing for the individual timekeeper, but it did set a baseline of priorities and tracking by the administrative staff. From there it was easy to identify the "problem children" of the firm.[1]
2. I allowed a wide variety of methods for timekeeping as long as such methods proved accurate and effective for the individual timekeeper. For example, some attorneys wrote the date, name of the client, and the start and completion times of every project on a yellow pad. Some used individual pages on a yellow pad for each new task of the day. Some simply wrote a list on one page per day, which included a *summary* of each task for a client performed that day. They either input more detail for each billing event right into their computer, which was connected to the billing system database in the office server, or turned in their handwritten timesheets for administrative staff to complete. I didn't care how it was done as long as it was done each day.
3. The timekeeping-and-billing system on their computers also allowed attorneys to turn on timers and identify each new client and new project

1. How this was performed evolved over the years as technology improved. Over the years, in-house computer networking and computerized timekeeping systems using real-time data bases became more cost-effective and useful, especially to the small firm that could not afford to spend $50,000 to custom design an in-house billing-and-timekeeping system.

they started. This timer was simply a new timeslip, fully filled in before the task was started, and could be turned off when that task was interrupted. Other timers could be turned on with new timeslips even if incomplete slips were still open. This method was easily adapted to the way the typical lawyer starts a project and gets interrupted several times during that project. Both the original and interrupting projects can be recorded and timed.[2]

4. We provided timekeepers with a list of codes making timekeeping entries easy and efficient. For example, if they input *tcc* into a time slip, the autotext *telephone conversations with client re* would appear. If they input *IC*, the autotext would be *Initial consultation with potential client to discuss all issues regarding divorce, review retainer agreement, and provide retainer requirements.* You get the picture. I tried to make it as easy as possible to input tasks directly into the timekeeping-and-billing system for each timekeeper.
5. The secret, if there is any for the timekeeper, is to begin the recording process *before* beginning the actual task, whether the task is a telephone conversation or a meeting with a client. (After all, it should be no surprise that you are going to have a meeting or a telephone conversation that you are initiating or that has been scheduled. So write it down just before starting, along with the starting time.) If using a yellow pad, this entails writing the client's name, date, and task description at the top of the page every time before jumping into the task itself. It also involves doing some recording immediately after the task before moving on to the next one. It is amazing how spending just a minute of time before and after a task jotting down a few words and the time can improve your timekeeping performance.
6. Most young attorneys are quite proficient on the computer. They can use the computerized timekeeping system with ease and take advantage of the customized codes in the system allowing for brief typing and resulting in detailed billing. I had one good attorney who was terrified of the timekeeping-and-billing system. (This attorney was banned from

2. A comprehensive survey of various case management and timekeeping/billing programs can be found at: http://www.americanbar.org/content/dam/aba/migrated/tech/ltrc/charts/pmtbchart.authcheckdam.pdf

all electrical appliances in the office after blowing up the microwave and the coffee machine, so her terror was justified.) And, although she could type proficiently, she was allowed to hand write her timekeeping entries. An administrative assistant was responsible for recording them first thing the next morning. The system worked, and the attorney was disciplined enough to keep her own time by hand.

7. Probably the best failsafe for timekeeping is not to leave the office until you have recorded all of your time for that day. Even then, if you are four hours behind, you may have trouble accurately recording your time. Jay Foonberg recommends using the Day-Timer system of writing in your book as each quarter hour is passed. Unfortunately, Day-Timers are not used as much now as in the old days, especially since computerized calendaring is also taking over the profession.
8. The good news is that if you use a computerized calendar or frequently e-mail to communicate with clients, staff, of other counsel, or third parties, and both synchronize to your computer and your smartphone, you have at least two other sources to review at the end of the day to recall what you have done. Every e-mail in your Sent box is a source for work accomplished, and the time, date, and client are already indicated in the e-mail.
9. Also consider your landline telephone and its capabilities for recording the time of phone calls. Many of these can be connected to your firm's timekeeping-and-billing system to automatically record the time, date, and client for whom you are calling.
10. An obvious source is an administrative assistant or legal assistant with whom you work closely. Ask to look at that person's time for the day, or ask the person to help you recall what you did that day. Remember, a supportive administrative or legal assistant's job frequently revolves around your job. They may inadvertently keep track of what you do better than you.

Billing

Most law firms today, large and small, begin the billing *production* process once the time period for the billing cycle has ended. It usually takes them a full month (or more) to complete this process and have the bills ready to send to clients. Once again, this has been the way it's usually been done, and no one seems to question whether there just might be a better way to avoid having earned income sit in a trust account for thirty to forty-five days, or worse, simply not bill a client for thirty (or more) days after work is complete. Can you imagine buying a book on Amazon.com, or buying food at the grocery store, and not being billed for a month? Why is it that law firms think that this is okay for only them? Well, I suspect that again tradition (or perhaps bad habit) is hard to break. Or perhaps their focus and creativity has been directed to their craft, and not this boring admin stuff. After all, their education, skills, and genius have been in the legal area, not the administrative area.

I had struggled for years trying to balance my time between my client or case deadlines and the necessary task of getting those pesky bills out in a timely manner. It had never occurred to me to make the billing process a priority. For me, it was always way down the priority list, after the obligations I had made to my clients were complete. The problem was, my services were never complete.

Around this time, my colleagues began to notice my proficiency on computers, and requests began coming in for me to assist other lawyers to upgrade their systems so that they could do some of the things they had heard I was doing.

I was installing a new computer system into a small law firm. (I did this as more of a hobby than a real business.) The firm was headed by a sole practitioner who wore only monogrammed French cuffs and the largest eighteen-carat gold Rolex I had ever seen. (I guess he needed a large watch because if it were any smaller, you would not notice it under the French cuffs.) He also drove a beautiful Mercedes and belonged to the most prestigious country club in Hawaii. His hourly billing rate was double mine at that time.

When we got around to discussing installation of a new computerized timekeeping-and-billing system, he informed me that when the calendar month was over, all legal work in his firm stopped and the entire personnel of the firm was dedicated to getting out the bills. That usually took his firm two full days. (This is *not* what I recommend you do, since this attorney lost twelve to fifteen hours of billable time doing it this way every month. At $350 per hour, you do the math.) However, the seeds of my system were born that day when I realized that the end of every billing cycle was predictable (duh), and hence the process could be scheduled and ultimately systematized so that nothing was left to chance. Why not actually schedule time for every component of that production every single month for anyone involved in the production of the bills? In other words, we knew it was coming, so why weren't we hardwiring it into our calendars ahead of time so we could devote the required time to produce and send the bills out?

The answer to this question became the bedrock of my entire integrated system of timekeeping, billing, and collections.

Computerized Billing Program

We have already covered the basics for the lawyers or legal assistants to be as efficient and effective as possible in keeping their time. The very next step is inputting their time into the computerized billing system. Most time-and billing-applications (software) do this automatically. That is, when a billing person calls up a computerized timeslip onto the computer screen, that timeslip is located in a server (hard drive) that contains all the timeslips opened by every billing personnel in the office. It's usually referred to as the database of the timeslips. In a database, all the information can be sorted in many useful ways at the push of a button. For example, you can sort slips by day or week (or any other time period to see how much was billed during that period), or by biller. This way, you can see how each billing employee (including yourself) is doing. And, of course, slips can be sorted by client, which, with one-time formatting, will result in a client billing worksheet (which works like a draft bill) and eventually a final bill, ready to be sent out (preferably by e-mail), complete with costs, expenses, and trust account transfers and balances.

Personnel Assignments

Probably the most important thing you can do to make this process efficient is to put one person in charge of getting the bills out and setting up the resulting transfer of money from the client trust account into your law firm business account. In small law firms, this responsibility usually lies with the office manager or lead administrative assistant. He or she will enlist other members of the administrative staff to assist in the assembly, proofing, and production of the monthly bills. This process includes retrieving copy costs from the copy machine and inputting any other expenditures made on behalf of the client into the billing program. Again, most firms begin this process at the end of the billing period. My staff does this input weekly, so that at the end of the month, there is only one week of miscellaneous data to be input before the bills are ready for review. The exception to this is the copy costs, which are derived from the copy machine and accumulated during the previous month. The totals are then cleared for the next billing period. It only makes sense to input copying costs once a month.

The other important part of this system is to schedule your and other lead attorneys' time each month to review each billing worksheet for errors, inefficiencies, write-offs, or any other changes needed before the bill is ready to send.

This is key.

You as owner, or other lead attorneys, will act as a bottleneck in the billing process if this is not scheduled and performed on a timely basis. Usually, I spend one evening per month performing this function, and get the agreement of other responsible attorneys to do the same. So, when the billing worksheets are produced and given to the reviewing attorneys, they take them home and review them one evening each month. They let family members know in advance that they need to be left alone for a few hours after dinner or that they will be late for dinner. This way, no time is lost between the production of the billing worksheets and their review and corrections. In most law firms, this process takes several weeks!

I do not let associates review their own billing worksheets unless they have matured in years and experience and I trust their perspective. The reason is that the reviewing attorney has the ability to write-off time or discount their own billing and billing done by those that they supervise. This is a delicate operation that takes into consideration overall efficiency of the firm and the particular efficiency of the personnel under the authority of the reviewing attorney.

It also serves the purpose of reviewing an attorney's billing and work habits. Once the reviewing attorney has developed the larger picture, adjustments can be made to the bill that may or may not be shown to the client. We never add time to a bill. We frequently subtract it and show that to the client as part of a courtesy or efficiency discount. Such discounts frequently have long-term PR value. It is our way of striking a balance between value billing and hourly billing.

Reductions in time billed also have a potentially negative effect on the billing person whose billable work is reduced. That person may have recorded 160 billable hours that month but the firm only billed 135 of those hours. If there are frequent or substantial reductions in the billable hours for a person, the situation and potential remedies will be discussed as part of the annual review. If the discounts are steep or chronic, it becomes a serious problem, and it will be discussed much sooner with the billing person.

The next day, the corrected billing worksheets are given to back to the office manager for delegation to other administrative assistant(s) to make all the changes indicated (usually in red) by the reviewing attorney. The administrative assistants are told to indicate a mark on the hard copy next to each change made in the billing worksheet to indicate that they incorporated every change requested by the reviewing attorney into the billing program.

Once this process is complete, the bills are ready to be finalized and set out.

Most clients have e-mail. As a result, most bills can be sent digitally to the client and avoid the costly and time-consuming paper process of printing, copying, envelop-stuffing, stamping, and mailing. For those clients without e-mail, this latter, old-fashioned process applies. Luckily, nowadays, that should apply to less than ten percent of your monthly billing statements.

Upon the "mailing" of client bills, the office manager can produce a list of clients and respective client trust account balances and transfers to the law firm's business account. A final review by the owner is a good idea to avoid any improper trust transfers. During this review it is easy to spot incorrect bookkeeping entries that result in incorrect bank balances or transfers. One this review has been completed, the owner should approve the trust account transfers. Then the office manager can make these transfers in a matter of seconds through the firm's online bank accounts. (It is actually one single bank transaction, from the client's trust account to the firm's business account.) The billing program (and resulting bookkeeping programs) will indicate each trust account transfer, client-by-client, in this single bank transaction. It will also automatically produce for you the aging accounts receivable analysis for the month so you can see instantly which, if any, clients are beginning to fall behind on their account balances.

From beginning to end, this process can be completed within two days of the end of the billing period. Any law firm that institutes this process, has after it had been taking the usual thirty to forty-five days, will now have an extra month's income immediately! (Let that sink in for a minute.)

Beware, however, that the first time you do this may be within a few days after your last bills were sent out. (That is, the ones you previously had been taking thirty to forty-five days to produce.) In order to avoid the appearance of billing your client twice for the same month, you may want to introduce this new system gradually by sending the client a notice that you are implementing a more efficient billing system which will result in their receiving their next month's invoices much closer to the previous billing period than before. You may want to delay two weeks before sending out your new bills just to give the clients some space between the last billing period under the old system and the new bills, which are almost up to the minute. Then, perhaps delay one week after the next month, with no delay the third month.

Either way, your firm will experience thirteen billing periods in the year following institution of your new billing system instead of twelve, providing an additional 8.33% revenue for the year (one month's average billing)! How much is that worth to your firm? In addition, you will be made aware of any client payment or cash-flow problems, that affect their payments, a month earlier than you used to. This process avoids the situation of working an additional month before you find out that a client cannot pay you. How much will this early awareness save you each year?

Accounts Receivable

Status Call to Client

As indicated in the retainer agreement, your clients have agreed to pay your invoices (or in cases where there are trust balances, to replenish the trust transfer) within ten days of receipt of their bills. On the eleventh day, the office manager is scheduled (on a computerized calendar with pop-up alerts, set to repeat on the same day every month) to begin calling clients who have not paid their invoiced amount, or replenished their trust account to its original balance, to inquire into the status of their payments.

This is an initial, friendly, touch-base call, which serves as both a reminder to those disorganized clients who forgot to pay their lawyer's bill, as well as notice to those who may have cash-flow challenges or received a bill much larger than expected. Either way, a single day should not go by before the office manager starts this process. It should take no longer that a couple of days for this process to be completed and may be split between the office manager and one or two administrative assistants if needed to complete this task within a couple of days.

As an added note, the lawyer should never make this call to his or her own client because the lawyer is too close to the client to be objective. Also, many lawyers become attached to and protective of their clients. Making a collection-type call places the lawyer in a position of divided loyalties. Better to have an objective third party who only answers to the boss and has no personal relationship with the client make the call. After all, this is a business arrangement and needs to be treated as such. At the same time, the caller should be polite and sensitive to the client's problems or concerns.

This is *not* a bill-collection call. It is just a status call, the results of which must be transmitted to the owner immediately after it has been made. Part of the call may entail a discussion regarding the client's cash-flow challenges, the client's concerns regarding any aspect of his or her case, or any other subject the client brings up. Regardless, the office manager or assistant making the call needs to ask specifically if there is a problem with making the payment as agreed in the client's retainer agreement. Then the office manager needs to listen carefully (without arguing) and pay particular attention to any concerns or challenges the client expresses. If the opportunity presents itself, the office manager may help the client brainstorm solutions to any financial challenges. In either case, whether client focused or firm focused, the office manager or assistant is to take clear notes and assure the client that he or she will meet with the boss and discuss this matter to seek resolution. No commitments should be made by the office manager during the call other than to get back to the client after the meeting with the boss. If the focus of the client is solely on cash-flow challenges, over time the office manager or assistant will develop the skill to brainstorm alternate sources of payment, such as the client's friends or relatives, credit card charges, or installment payments to the law firm.

It is important to train an office manager or assistant to make these calls. Your training should include the following goals:

1. communicating to the client that a payment is due
2. listening for any response other than the payment will be made and noting that response for communication to the owner
3. asking clarifying questions to get a clearer picture of the client's concerns, either personal financial concerns or concerns with the bill or services received
4. if appropriate (that is, if, in the clarifying process, the client indicates he or she needs to borrow money, charge the amount owed on a credit card, or use any other method of payment other than sending a check immediately), assist the client in planning and implementing the tasks needed to make payment. The assistant should do this even if the client can only make partial payment and note the client's plan and calendar the plan (if it involves a future date). This plan needs to be time specific, or it is not a real plan. If the client resists committing to a particular date, the assistant should back off and simply note that in a report to the owner.

It is more important to have an organized, detail-oriented, worker-bee type of person fill this role than an office manager or assistant with good communication skills who may be less detailed oriented. Each detail left out costs the firm money. (More about placing the right employee in the right job is in Chapter 5.)

Once all calls have been made and the status communicated to the owner in writing (via e-mail, for example), the owner then meets with the office manager to address any potential problems with clients paying their bills. Just like the monthly repeated date for making these calls, this meeting should be calendared on a repeat basis every month and should only be moved or postponed if the owner is in trial. (Even if the owner is on vacation or out of town, the meeting should take place. The owner can retrieve the e-mail on his smartphone or laptop and discuss each client over the telephone with the office manager.) If calendared a year in advance, the attorney can even avoid conflicts caused by other matters such as trials or depositions since the attorney can indicate that he or she is already committed on those prescheduled dates.

The sooner the owner realizes there may be a concern about the client's fulfilling his or her contractual responsibilities, the better and easier it will be to address it. If the firm is still using the outdated, traditional system of sending bills (where it has taken a month or so just to get the bills out), the first time the owner is even aware of a client's concerns or cash flow challenges is thirty to forty-five days, at best, *after* an *additional* month's work has been done. That means that you or your other attorneys or staff have continued business as usual for almost two months completely unaware of the client's potential inability to pay the bills or the client's concerns with the firm's handling of their case. *This delay alone is a systemic flaw in these traditional billing systems that contributes to the ever-increasing accounts receivables, or worse, deteriorating client relations experienced by law firms.*

Before we get to the owner's job after receiving this monthly report from the office manager or assistant, it should be noted that just making these calls on a timely, periodic basis will increase your cash flow by anywhere from ten to twenty-five percent per month. For a firm of three lawyers and two legal assistants, this amount could be $7,000 to $17,500 per month! This amount of extra cash flowing through the firm (and ultimately into your profit) justifies hiring an extra administrative assistant who is devoted full time to accounts receivable. However, in a firm this size, you won't need even one-fourth of this assistant's time for this task. *In other words, it is incredibly cost-effective to employ the staff for this task.* Any firm that does not have adequate staffing to accomplish these important tasks is penny wise and pound foolish. It is losing money every month in which accounts receivable are treated on an ad hoc or low priority basis.

This is what most small firms do, and it is also the reason these firms rarely grow in size or increase their earnings.

Owner's Duties

Now it is the owner's turn to make decisions based on the office manager's report of telephone conversations with the clients.

The owner is up to date on the status of all cases since he or she has attended the weekly case-review meeting the previous Friday. The owner brings the updated chart from the case-review meeting to the meeting with the office manager or assistant who made the ten-day status calls to the clients.

The first piece of information the owner receives is how much additional revenue (from all clients) can be expected shortly, which is on top of the revenue already received from the client trust transfer made when the bills were sent out. This financial information will give the owner an accurate picture of the end-of-the-month cash flow early enough in the month to know if the firm needs to tap into its bank line of credit. No surprises, no waiting for the mail to see if the firm can meet the monthly nut. No last minute stress. Or, put more optimistically, the owner is able to determine if there is surplus cash flow from which to put money aside for future equipment purchases, future hiring, or just a bonus for the owner or a deserving employee.

Secondly, the owner needs to decide how to respond to clients who are unable to reimburse their trust accounts or pay the firm what is owed. (Nothing needs to be done with clients who are paid up or whose trust balances are sufficient to cover the previous month's billings.) This meeting concerns active cases only where a bill went out less than two weeks ago. Clients who have owed money for more than thirty days are discussed in the next section.

It is not that difficult to have a general idea of how much work needs to be done in a particular case and compare that to the client's current financial situation. After all, you should have a clear picture of the client's asset and debt situation by now, and you have a current case-status report with which to compare it. Based on the individual reports presented by your office manager, you will need to decide whether you need to call the client yourself or delegate that responsibility to the office manager or assistant with specific recommendations regarding borrowing, selling, or getting additional help to pay the amount owed to the firm. You may also need to explain to the client why his or her bill is much larger than expected. Most of the time clients know this information as they have been involved in a motion or other discovery process or because you simply have done a good job copying the client on all correspondence and pleadings in their case. But many times, clients do not have any idea how much time was needed to perform last month's needed tasks. You may need to explain this to them. Also, you may want to revise the latest bill and write off some time based on an inordinate amount of time spent on a task by an associate or legal assistant that was missed in the billing worksheet review process. This write-off capability should be used on a regular basis as the second part of your modified value-billing approach to cases. It is a matter of fairness and good client relations, and it can indicate which associates or legal assistants consistently have their time written off. This may be a further indication of padded bills or inefficiency on the part of your staff.

This is my approach to all of the discussions relating to value billing. When one has a pure litigation practice, it is almost impossible to predict what the fee will be, especially in family law cases. Hence, pure value-billing or fixed-fee cases are by definition unfair to either you or the client. Either you underestimate, or, in an effort to protect yourself, overestimate and as a result, may not get the work. That's why it is better to use hourly-rate billing and maintain a trust between client and lawyer, where the lawyer is not arrogant or naive to assume all bills are sacrosanct or received with good feeling by the client. This trust involves a delicate dance between attorney and client. It is not unlike the delicate dance of marriage negotiation where give and take on issues that are more important to one spouse do not involve direct confrontation or accusation of malfeasance. Building this trust requires frank discussions of client's perceptions of the case balanced by the lawyer's perspective on the time needed to accomplish a task or the changing nature of the case. Some value-billing advocates recommend that clients sign change orders, much like the change orders that are signed in a construction project. This is a great idea and should always be part of the case-review process when an unanticipated and undiscussed change in the direction of a case occurs. That is, once a case takes an unexpected turn involving additional discovery, for example, the client should be brought in to discuss it and to address it financially or otherwise. This is good client communication, as well as preventive medicine for the accounts receivable blues.

Withdrawal from Representation

As I stated at the beginning of this chapter, one of the bedrock concepts of this system is the willingness of the firm to withdraw from representing a client who fails to fulfill the obligations under the firm's retainer agreement.[3]

Just the mere discipline of having a system to make this decision will improve the firm's cash flow and each attorney's effective billing rate (EBR)[4] although I have seen the system sabotaged by a particular attorney's unwillingness to press a client for alternative payment arrangements or to withdraw from representation. This behavior usually results from over-identification with the client and usually (but not always) comes from an attorney who will not experience the financial repercussions of working for a client for free. (Caveat: Tying an individual attorney's compensation directly to revenue produced may produce other, even more undesirable results which have little to do with quality legal work or what is best for the client.) Each attorney's EBR should be calculated monthly as one of many factors in evaluating that attorney's performance. A consistently low EBR can reveal many things, from poor client selection to overbilling to various inefficiencies of the attorney. Using the attorney's EBR as one criteria in that attorney's evaluation helps cure the attorney's over-identification with the client, which usually accompanies poor business practices.

The firm should *consider* withdrawal from representing a client once:

1. a client has consistently failed to fulfill his or her obligations under the retainer agreement, or
2. it becomes clear from the unfolding of the case that the client has misrepresented the complexities or depth of the conflict involved in the case, and does not have a credible explanation for this misrepresentation, or

---

3. This is not as easy as it sounds, nor should it become mechanical or be strictly followed. There are at least two (and probably more) reasons for this. First, absolute adherence to a strict rule to withdraw from representing a client may run afoul of ethical rules if it becomes clear that part of your firm's business practices involves taking cases from clients who predictably may not be able to keep current on their bills. Second, every case and client circumstance is unique. Strict withdrawal may be bad public relations and simply insensitive to clients whose cases you can finish without a serious effect on your cash flow.

4. See Chapter 9.

3. the client simply cannot provide ongoing financial support, and you estimate that the firm's future financing of the case will cause undue financial harm to the firm (e.g., the client will never be able to pay the firm and such a write-off is too much for the firm to bear).

The weekly case-review process along with the monthly meeting by the firm owner and the office manager will result in the clear identification of the cases and clients that fit into the above categories. Once the client is identified and all efforts have been exhausted to assist the client in meeting his or her obligations, the firm's owner either must decide to support the case or withdraw from representing the client. Since withdrawing from representing a client is perfunctory in most jurisdictions, there is little to be said about it. Most important is to insure that your withdrawal does not come at a critical place in the litigation or life of the case (such as being too close to trial if there is one scheduled); otherwise it could harm the client's case or threaten your success in withdrawal. Most jurisdictions' ethical codes include provisions that discourage any action by counsel that may adversely affect their clients' cases. Withdrawing from representing a client too late in a case can be considered one of these ethical violations.

Supporting the case usually means advancing all future costs involved in the case, as well as basically financing the remaining billing until some later date. If the case should result in the client's receipt of funds, either from the opposing party or from the sale of an asset, you may try to get the client's agreement to the firm's continued representation, in exchange for agreeing to insure payment of your fees. These terms are already included in my sample retainer agreement and have been successful on many occasions in gaining court orders directing payment to my firm from third parties (such as escrow companies or financial institutions), or the terms act as escrow instructions to be paid out of the sale of an asset.

Bringing in a third party to guaranty payment is also another option. Responsible review of a third party's financial resources or credit may be required. If the third party has no income or assets from which you may collect, a guaranty may not have any value.

Many jurisdictions allow a charging lien by the attorney if requested as part of the motion to withdraw. This may be your only recourse if you have a client who will not agree to provide you security on your fees. A court order in the form of a charging lien should solve this problem.

Collection Actions

Only after you have severed the attorney-client relationship can you take legal action to collect sums owed to you. Before you do, however, there are many caveats you should be aware of before deciding on this course of action.

First, your errors-and-omissions carrier may discourage any actions against former clients as they may feel that legal actions give rise to counterclaims of professional negligence. Therefore, it is critical that your review of the case involve an errors-and-omissions audit—*before* referring the case to collection counsel—to insure the client has no counterclaims. But look, this is America, the land of the lawsuit. Any client may choose to assert claims no matter how frivolous, and therefore may decide to counterclaim with no justifications whatsoever. And that client may even find an attorney to support such a frivolous claim. Hence, it is your call whether you agree to proceed once given the green light by collections counsel. If collections counsel assesses weaknesses in your case that may give rise to counterclaims, it may not be advisable to pursue any collection action. You are merely buying yourself misery and more distractions from running your practice.

Second, it (almost) goes without saying, do not prosecute these collections actions yourself. Hire a skilled collections attorney who also has experience in post-judgment execution such as attachment of assets, wage or bank garnishee actions, or tracing of assets. The additional benefit of using skilled counsel (other than the obvious objectivity you'll need, and additional skill you will benefit from) is that collections counsel are usually allowed to add attorneys' fees to your initial claim based upon your jurisdiction's assumpsit statutes. This can, in whole or in part, pay for counsel's fees charged to you. Provisions in your retainer agreement for payment of reasonable attorney's fees in cases of litigation are discretionary by the court; assumpsit statutory fees are not.

Third, it is advisable to set a threshold value of cases below which you will not pursue a collection action, for example, clients who owe you less than $5,000 or $10,000 or who have no visible means of producing income or no assets from which to collect. Do this in conjunction with collections counsel with the goal of not having to pay unnecessary legal fees pursuing a judgment that has little likelihood of being satisfied.

I developed a good relationship with collections counsel who handled dozens of cases over a period of years for my firm. Because of this, few errors in judgment were made in suing clients. It was his job to prepare the cases for trial, and all I had to do was testify. Expectations of effort by him and participation by me became second nature. The judges also were impressed by our preparation, documentation, and succinct presentation of our cases. I received judgments, which included statutory awards of attorney's fees and costs, on every collection action filed but one. I collected, mostly by way of wage or bank account garnishment, on approximately ninety percent of these judgments.

5

HOW TO CHOOSE YOUR EMPLOYEES WELL

Find the Best People You Can Afford

In my early years as a sole practitioner, I was fortunate enough to hire a person whose skills expanded with my practice. This person handled all administrative duties except bookkeeping. For a few years, until Quicken and QuickBooks came out, and before the advent of the Macintosh computer, I paid a bookkeeping service to produce monthly financial statements and balance sheets. Other than that, my sole employee performed the duties of receptionist, secretary, filing clerk, administrative assistant, accounts receivable and payable clerk, and paralegal. As my practice grew, each of these duties expanded and began to be performed by individual staff as money and volume increased. The written descriptions of my employee's duties and tasks became the basis for identifying the kinds of skills that were needed when looking for new employees, as well as for detailed job descriptions used to train employees. I will be ever grateful for this amazing employee who worked for me for my first ten years in practice. She is now the office manager for a major firm of over fifty attorneys.

Finding skilled, well-qualified support staff in the legal profession where I practiced was not that difficult. There were many good employees out there who were unhappy and felt unsupported or underpaid in their present positions. Advertising, or putting the word out, that I was looking for a specific skill set or position usually yielded many good applicants.

Unfortunately, I had no skill set in the hiring process. I did have the benefit of having been an employee and wanting to eliminate many of the things I disliked about being an employee—such as bosses who did not really provide support, poor or complete lack of training, lack of appreciation or reward for exceptional effort, and low pay. I had vowed that if I ever owned my own business, I would make sure I would provide an environment where my employees never experienced these things. Ultimately, I accomplished all of these things. The only problem was, I did not know how to hire the right employee for the right job. I also failed to scrutinize job applicants properly to insure that, in exchange for good working conditions and top salaries and benefits, they would work hard and contribute to the goals and mission of my law firm. But there were problems: I had no written mission statement for them to subscribe to, and I had no system for matching personality types with job descriptions. I just sort of winged it for a long time and had spotty and inconsistent results.

When I finally got tired of replacing at least one employee every year, I hired a business coach who helped me develop a mission statement and operating values for everyone at the firm.[1] The business coach also assisted me in the hiring process by having finalists whom I had interviewed tested online to make sure they were a right fit for the job.

Hiring the Right Person for the Right Job

I had two consecutive employees in the intake coordinator's position who failed miserably on the job and caused a loss of firm morale, as well as a loss of business until I discovered, almost inadvertently, what they were doing. Nonexistent hiring practice and poor management and supervision on my part allowed these employees to suffer in a position not suited to their skill set or personality type, and finally resulted in the firing of one and the resignation (out of frustration) of the other. Since the intake coordinator position was the first line of contact with potential or existing clients, I thought I needed

1. A copy of my firm's mission statement is attached as Appendix 3. It will be dealt with in more detail in Chapter 11.

a person who had good people skills. Both of these employees had wonderful empathy with people they spoke to, but neither could keep up with the paperwork involved in tracking calls or moving documents or information throughout the firm without making a mess of it. One of them was so empathetic with potential clients that she discouraged many of them from hiring our firm because she felt so guilty asking these suffering people for money. She figured that our firm was just too expensive or that the potential client was in such distress that telling them that they had to fill out paperwork and pay us $150 to have an appointment was just too onerous and mean. She actually blurted this out in a staff meeting.

That was her last day that involved any client contact.

Because I had not kept up on the number of phone calls the firm was receiving (since she was not recording all the calls coming in as part of her job), I had failed to notice a huge drop in new clients for over a two-month period. She was replaced by someone to whom it was made clear that the goal was to bring clients in the door, while at the same time, to assist in a process of filtering out clients that were not a good fit for the firm. This employee was also an empathetic listener, but she also couldn't keep up with paperwork, which involved sending out forms for potential clients to fill out before appearing for an appointment. (See the job description of the intake coordinator in Chapter 1.) After she was fired (for other reasons), I found out that she was continually overwhelmed and pleaded with other employees to help her complete her work daily.

It was at this point that my most senior attorney and my wife (who is a CPA) approached me with a novel idea: that they take over the hiring process. They gently informed me that of the many skills I exhibited as an attorney and business manager, hiring was not one of them. They could see that for me the hiring process was one of selling the benefits of working at such an incredible firm rather than what it should be, one of carefully scrutinizing applicants for a given job opening. Once they took over the hiring process, once we had a firm mission statement in place, and once finalists were tested for their skill strengths, our hiring process and overall staff quality improved greatly. When you combine proper hiring with proper employee treatment, you get great results on many levels.

For example, after using skilled interviewers to cull through job applications and interview candidates for the intake coordinator's position, and having the position filled not by a people person, but by an organized, diligent worker to whom we could teach the applicable interviewing skills for the job, we found a tremendous replacement for the position.

After this person worked at the firm for two weeks, she asked to speak with me privately. I thought that she had decided that the job was not a good fit for her and was about to give me notice of her leaving. The first thing she did was to show me the job description given to her as part of her training and ask, "Is this the entire job description?" I responded positively and asked why. She said, "Because this only takes me about two hours a day. I need more work to do." Not only was this person doing a flawless job, but she did it in about one-fourth the time it took two previous employees to do. I knew we had chosen the right person for the job! As the firm expanded, this person moved into another administrative and client-contact position and trained her replacement. The system was working well.

Here's what you need to do to get the right person for the right job:

1. Have a detailed job description prepared for every position in the firm. If you don't have job descriptions, have each current employee jot down over a period of a week or two every distinct task he or she accomplishes as it is accomplished. If there are tasks that must be done daily, they should be noted separately. Have employees also describe what skills they use to accomplish these tasks, such as typing (keyboarding), spreadsheet preparation, or good listening or organizational skills. Then have the employees trade these job descriptions with each other to get feedback, suggested additions, or modifications to sharpen up the job descriptions. If you already have a good office manager or human resources person capable of detailed analysis, have that person meet with each employee to review the job description, ask questions about the work flow and tasks, and make modifications as necessary. This document can and should be revised every year to reflect changes in tasks and responsibilities as the firm changes or grows and tasks are shared or re-allocated.
2. Have a professional interviewer cull through the resumes and perform the initial interviews of only the most promising candidates. If you have

to outsource this job, it is well worth the money. I know you are a highly intelligent attorney with a myriad of skills, but let me tell you, you may not have a clue of what is involved with interviewing or hiring new employees. I didn't. Once I acknowledged this, stopped doing most of the interviewing myself, and got involved only at the tail end of the hiring process, the quality of my workforce improved dramatically.

3. Have final candidates take an online test to make sure they have the correct personality profile for the job for which they are applying. There are several online testing services that provide testing and even interview guidance. It is well worth the money and will go a long way to prevent you from placing the wrong person in the wrong job.[2]

Small Firm Job Combinations

1. Office Manager

Most small firms cannot afford to have a dedicated employee for each discrete job description or department. Hence, your office manager will typically fulfill the position of human resources manager (HR), accounts payable (AP) and accounts receivable (AR), as well as bookkeeper and perhaps supervisor in charge of facilitating the monthly billing process. You'll notice that all functions, except the HR function, are related to the firm's financial resources and revenue generation. So, it makes sense that one person should be in charge of these particular responsibilities until you grow to a point where you can afford to share these duties among two or more employees. Probably the most critical skills required for this position are attention to detail and organizational skills related to detailed record keeping.

2. Administrative Assistant (AA)

Every professional baseball team usually has one player that can play all infield or all outfield positions. They are typically referred to as utility players. The practice of law in a small law firm is no different. The administrative assistant is a skilled employee who should be able to perform a myriad of tasks to assist either the legal assistants, the attorneys, or the office manager

2. I primarily used the DISC Test. Two services that provide the test, as well as related services are http://www.discprofile.com/cart/ or, https://www.onlinedisc.com/

in meeting their responsibilities. An AA is usually charged with completing the administrative, non-technical parts of tasks, such as keyboarding, copying and assembling documents, organizing files, and drafting and proofing or reviewing documents before they are finalized and mailed, e-mailed, or filed in court. Different in scope from the legal assistant (described below) who is the responsible, go-to person for a given case, the AA can work on more than one case to assist a legal assistant or attorney with ad hoc tasks. The AA can also assist the office manager throughout the month with inputting and preparing the invoices that should go out within days of the end of any billing period (see Chapter 4). An AA should also be fully trained to take over the intake coordinator's position at a moment's notice due to illness, vacations, or lunchtime.

This position is the most flexible and requires a whole host of technical skills not found in lawyers or legal assistants. Hence, the AA should have the primary personality trait of getting satisfaction from being a worker bee. Once the tasks are clearly set out for this type of employee, leave the AA alone to do the jobs and avoid interfering with the that person's progress.

3. Intake Coordinator

I have covered the general job description of the intake coordinator in Chapter 1 as that person who is basically the gatekeeper of all information coming in to the firm, whether by telephone, mail, e-mail, or fax. The coordinator receives this information, records it, and distributes it. For potential clients, the coordinator performs the tasks described in Chapter 1 to move those potential clients from a voice on the phone to the initial interview with an attorney. Or by simply following the system, the coordinator weeds out undesirable potential clients. This person must have good organizational and record-keeping skills.

4. Legal Assistant (LA) or Paralegal

This person must have skills developed from either a certified paralegal course of study or years of experience in a particular field of law, or both, to be able to function as a true paralegal. The only limits of what a paralegal can do are proscribed by legal and ethical rules governing the practice of law in your jurisdiction. Paralegals cannot take depositions, but they can prepare deposition questions and summarize deposition transcripts. They can supervise discovery and prepare initial drafts of interrogatories, requests for production, and subpoenas. They cannot appear in court, but they can be invaluable in preparing an attorney for court by accomplishing tasks such as preparation of exhibits and preparation of direct and cross-examination questions. They cannot sign legal documents as an attorney, but they can prepare drafts of those documents for an attorney's review.

In my firm, the legal assistant was also the person responsible for keeping the file up to date daily, as well as the person in charge of the knowledge and calendaring of all case deadlines. However, the lead attorney is still ultimately responsible to the client for everything in the case. And finally, the legal assistant is a good liaison between the client and the attorney for relaying messages in either direction and for case coordination between client, attorney, and anyone else involved in the case. In our firm, the more technical tasks performed by the legal assistant were typically delegated to an administrative assistant who reported to one or more legal assistants. The legal work requiring some substantive or procedural work is reserved for legal assistants.[3]

Once you have placed the right persons in the right positions, you have built the foundation for a competent, stable, and vital work force. Competent because you have matched personality or work style with skills required in the job that matches that style. Stable because you have increased the probabilities that that employee will perform at a level that will provide them and you with satisfaction with their work. And vital because any well-performing firm or workforce will provide new opportunities and goals for its employees to strive for and reach, with accompanying rewards and a sense of pride.

However, once employees are on the job, their proper care and nurturing will complete the combination needed to change your major focus from employee challenges to employee successes and accomplishments. What are the major points in keeping a good employee motivated and happy and performing at a high level? Read on.

3. A sample job description for a paralegal or legal assistant is attached as Appendix 4.

6

HOW TO TREAT YOUR EMPLOYEES WELL

Setting the Foundation for a Competent, Stable, and Vital Work Force

Your responsibility to your employees is twofold:

First, it is your responsibility to communicate to your employees exactly what you expect from them, both in terms of skills exhibited and expected performance and results.

Second, it is your responsibility to support and motivate your employees in their quest to improve their skills and performance as they work to achieve the firm's goals. *Catch them doing something right* is a relatively recent cliché that indicates where your focus should be. I would simply tell my employees that *my* job, as far as they were concerned, was to support them in doing *their* job in the best, most efficient manner possible. I told them they could test me on this anytime, to see if this were really true or not. All they had to do was request a new office chair, desk, or computer and justify to me why this new piece of equipment or this weekly night-school course would improve their performance, and I would gladly pay for it.

That's it!

This approach formed a marvelously positive foundation for the employer-employee relationship. Once employees are convinced that you are there to support them to be the best they could be, there is no end to their work ethic or creativity.

On the other hand, if employees feel that you focus on what they do wrong or that you "motivate" by fear, they will never perform to their highest potential and will be motivated by a variety of other hidden goals (such as hiding mistakes), rather than the goals of your firm or the quality of their work. When their goals are ultimately in conflict with those of the firm (and they will be), employees will quit or be fired (or should be fired).

Many attorneys never talk to employees about their own work or challenges because they either think these matters are irrelevant to the employee's job, or they misunderstand the value of transparency. On the contrary, once a properly placed employee gets to know what the firm is trying to do, both in a micro sense (as in any particular case or how the quality of their work affects other employees), and in a macro sense (as in how the quality of their work fits in to the firm's overall goals and systems as indicated in its mission statement), the employee will figure out how to improve his or her performance and contribute to the firm's overall goals. If employees believe that you've got their back, they will stretch and push towards the firm's goals and stay consistent with the firm's mission. They will rightly feel that they are part of a team and have the potential to see their hard work as part of something bigger than themselves.

Breaking this down into workable parts and addressing them in a systematic way, an employee can only perform to his or her full potential if he or she understands:

1. The current job description (i.e., what specific duties you expect from the employee) and
2. the evaluation process (i.e., how their performance is evaluated) and
3. training and compensation (i.e., how your system supports and rewards improvement in the performance of work duties) and
4. the firm's mission statement (and how what employees do contributes to the overall mission of the firm).

Let's explore each of these.

The Job Description

As alluded to in the previous chapter, a job description, complete with specific duties and skills required to attain success on the job, is critical to hiring the best employees for the job. But more than that, it can serve both as a training guide as well as a checklist of duties and tasks to be performed.

As a training guide, the job description can thoroughly and efficiently guide the employee through a comprehensive training process. It can also identify the new employee's shortcomings, if any, so that specific training can be applied to address deficiencies in skills needed for excellence on the job. Additional in-house training can be scheduled to eliminate these gaps in skills. Or additional training may be outsourced for more in-depth, specialized skills, such as advanced word processing or spreadsheet skills.

There are three keys to keeping the job description relevant and vital for the employee. First, the job description must be periodically updated to reflect the realities of a changing, dynamic law practice. The update must include the employee's input as well as that of the employee's direct supervisor and the office manager. Second, specific tasks from the job description may be transferred to each case's various case-management checklists so that the employee can see the practical application of his or her duties. Completion of these tasks or duties can also be recorded in the calendar or on the case management checklist. Third, to support the employee from dropping the ball, any repetitive tasks can be calendared, complete with repeats and reminders for these duties. I cannot impress enough how important this last simple technological advance of electronic calendars has become. Not only can these tasks be calendared to repeat, but others can be invited to participate in the scheduling of tasks for a further failsafe in getting the job done.

Evaluation

Not unlike a child who looks for feedback from mom or dad on how they are doing, every employee wants, and you the employer owe, an honest assessment and evaluation of employee performance at the firm. When done in a fair, objective manner, evaluation forms the basis for salary increases, additional training, and promotions.

Each employee should be told when hired how he or she is going to be evaluated. On the first day of employment, each new employee should be given the firm's evaluation form, which will be filled in by both employee and employer on the first anniversary of the employee's employment at the firm. Why firms insist on keeping this part of the evaluation process a secret I'll never know. Maybe it has something to do with misperceptions of knowledge and power. Keeping employees in the dark about their evaluation process is counterproductive.

How does an employer expect an employee to have goals consistent with the firm if the employer hides the goal? Why should an employee have to guess or be surprised at how his or her performance will be evaluated for a year's time when you, the employer, can provide them a cheat sheet, designed to let them look behind the curtain, track their progress, and assess their performance in the same way the employer or supervisor does? No firm that I know of does this—except ours.

I've had employees tack this evaluation form to the walls in their workstations, so they can stay conscious of what specific traits and work will be evaluated on each anniversary of their employment.[1] Does this not make all the sense in the world?

Here's a good way to go about performing an annual, constructive employee evaluation:

1. Provide the employee with a blank form to fill out about two weeks before you plan on doing the evaluation. Fill one out yourself, either in consultation with the employee's direct supervisor, or, if the supervisor is up to the task, have him or her fill it out as well.
2. Set an appointment with the employee. At the appointment, make a copy of each filled-in form so that each of you have both completed forms.
3. Spend time discussing points of similarity and difference between the comments and the numerical ranking in each area of the form. The idea behind this meeting is to attempt to reconcile, or at a minimum, understand, each other's perspective on how the employee performed in the various areas designated in the form. Employees have told me how beneficial this discussion is to them.

1. A copy of a typical employee evaluation form is in Appendix 5.

4. One of the most important parts of the form is the goals. This is an area where specific improvements can be stated and measured for next year's evaluation. For example, if an employee has challenges in their punctuality, attendance, dress, writing style, grammar, or timekeeping, specific goals can be articulated that can be measured against next year's evaluation. Rather than be stated as a negative or criticism, they can be phrased as goals to be achieved, accompanied by a time-sensitive plan of action designed to reach that goal.
5. If you have already done your yearly budget analysis (see Chapter 9) and know how much you have allocated to raises and bonuses for the coming year, you are ready to present the employee with a salary increase. If not, let the employee know you will provide this information in a couple of days at most.
6. Finally, you and the employee should sign the evaluation forms, especially the one that includes goals for next year. The employee should be provided with a copy, and your copy goes into the employee's personnel file.

Training, Salaries, Bonuses, and Incentives

Training

Remember when I said that part of the employer's job was "to support and motivate your employees in their quest to improve their skills and performance?" This support begins with proper training but does not end there.

Several years ago, I remember reading about the superior products Japanese manufacturers were producing compared to those produced by American manufacturers and about the numerous studies of this difference. One of the studies pointed out that in many Japanese companies, the best employee in any area was charged with training all employees doing the same or similar tasks. In contrast, it was noted that in many American companies, once an employee was trained on the job (*if* he or she was trained), the newest employee was charged with training the next new employee, and so on down the line. The result was that several generations of training later, the training became diluted or completely unrecognizable as the training the first employee received. Once I learned that, I either trained each of my employees myself or had my best employees repeat the same training to each new employee. We never relegated such an important part of the employee's success to the least skilled or newest person in the office.

In addition to initial on-the-job training, there are many organizations that provide better training than we in the law business do, whether that training is in spreadsheets or word-processing magic or in pre-trial discovery strategies. Just as for attorneys, continuing education is critical for the success of your employees. If they are charged with looking for additional ways they can become more valuable to the firm, and they know you will support (pay for) it, they will always be on the lookout for it. That is exactly what you want. If your office manager has been getting human resources training from the local employer's council or chamber of commerce, he or she will be made aware of all kinds of appropriate employee training and courses.

Salaries

One of my all-time favorite legal assistants once asked to talk to me privately in my office. After we closed the door, he carefully and quietly informed me that he had been offered a job by another firm at a salary of $500 per month more than I was paying him. He made it clear that he loved working in our firm, but that he had a growing family (his wife had recently had their second child) and needed to consider them in his decision. He did *not* want to leave, he stressed, but he was wondering if I would consider giving him some type of raise, even though the anniversary of his employment had not arrived. This way, he explained, he could turn down the offer, which is what he wanted, and he could justify this decision to his wife. He added that he did not want to put me on the spot, and that I could take all the time I needed to respond.

I responded that I knew this other lawyer and that she was one of most disorganized lawyers I had met. I did not think he would enjoy working there. Her office was a dangerous mess and my paralegal would probably be charged with cleaning up years of unfiled documents in addition to his normal duties. I just thought he should know that. I then said that I would make some calls around town to see what a legal assistant with his level of skill and experience was being paid. If I found that he was in fact being underpaid, I would consider a raise. He was fine with that.

I then set out to do what I had promised. When I was finished, I found out that I was probably underpaying him by the amount he was offered in the new job. So a few days after our first conversation, I called him back in and told him what I had learned. I believed that he was stunned by my candor. I also assured him that he was a valuable member of the firm whom I did not want to lose. I offered to increase his salary by the same $500 monthly increase he was being offered by the other firm, but that he would forgo any end-of-the-year bonus and any raise on the next anniversary of his employment. I told him that it would not be fair to the other employees to give him more frequent raises than them, and I did not want to start an avalanche of employees asking for raises before their time. I asked him to keep this private for that reason.

The look on his face was one I will never forget. I thought this grown, reserved man was going to cry on the spot. He was absolutely surprised at my willingness to meet his other offer dollar for dollar, and not give him a hard time of it. He leapt up and almost jumped over my desk to shake hands with me and thank me vigorously. He is still an employee at the firm, and he is now in charge of supervising and training the other legal assistants.

The reason I tell this story is because compensation is a difficult issue to address. Nevertheless, in the law business, where a valuable employee can bring in revenue several times his or her salary and benefits, trying to shave an employee's salary to save a few bucks may be shortsighted and, in fact, counterproductive. Good, dedicated employees are what you are looking for, and in the long run, paying and rewarding productive behavior is the name of the game.

All of your employees should be classified into similar groups, and for each group, your office manager should keep a compensation range based on skills and years of experience. Online services and employer groups can provide this guidance. It is within this range that your new employees should be paid. On job applications, we ask what salary range the applicant is looking for. If the range is too low, we ignore it and pay them what we think they are worth. If it is too high, we let them know the best we can do according to what we consider their range, but that we will be willing to review this subject ninety days after the start of their employment. At that time, if they show exemplary skills, initiative, and performance, we may raise their salaries substantially, especially if their revenue production supports this approach.

Bonuses

We provide bonuses at two kinds of opportunities. The first is at the end of the year, and it is based on how the entire firm has done. The second is when we collect on a big case and the firm simultaneously celebrates this victory of sorts. Both bonuses are based on sound principles. The end-of-the-year bonus is part of my own planning process and marks a good time to reflect on what has happened during the previous year.

For everyone.

It also is a holiday time when a little extra cash is welcome by a salaried employee. I always provide this bonus check before Christmas (regardless of religious affiliation, which is none of my business) as an added help to my employees. I have even had to draw from my line of credit to do this, knowing that the loan may last no more than a week or so.

The victory bonus is a way of letting salaried employees know that they are really part of a winning team. It puts my money where my mouth is. Lip service is cheap. I can have nicely framed posters all over the office about teamwork and talk about it or send employees to seminars to teach them the value of teamwork. If I don't share the spoils of the results of good teamwork, it can look like and probably is just manipulative lip service.

If, on the other hand, the employee has seen others or has been previously rewarded for exemplary effort as part of a successful case, he or she will never forget that and will frequently work hard to replicate that success in future cases. In essence, you have given the employee a vested interest in the firm's success, case by case. The employee personally feels that he or she owns the cases and will behave accordingly. Instead of sharing the wealth, you could go out and buy yourself a new BMW after a financially rewarding case and give the employees nothing. I assure you this will be counterproductive. Employees want you to appear successful, but not at their expense. This is especially relevant to the employees who bill their time. They are acutely aware of the money they are producing for the firm. They will know when you are hoarding extra income at their expense, and they will resent it.

Incentives

Finally, I attempt to motivate employees with unexpected incentives, like gift cards or other valuable gifts, when that employee comes up with an idea or system or innovation that saves the firm money or increases our overall efficiency. These incentive gifts are for non-client matters. These gifts are given in front of all the employees, so peers can recognize each other's work and be motivated to continually think of ways to improve our firm.

I do *not* believe in the effectiveness of systems like employee of the month (or year) because this sets up what I believe is unhealthy competition between employees (rather than cooperation for a greater good) and always involves winners and losers. It also has little to do with the overall success of the firm, which I would like to have the employees be cognizant of so that again, they feel their efforts have contributed to achieving the firm's goals. Appreciation and acknowledgment of their efforts in these ways makes what they're doing in your firm have meaning beyond the regular paycheck.

The Firm's Mission Statement

For years I operated my law firm hanging on by my fingernails in order not to commit malpractice, blow any court deadlines, and hopefully make payroll and pay my office rent on time. It never occurred to me that I was operating the firm with a set of values or that the firm had a mission. Since I was unaware of, or had never consciously articulated, what these values were or what our firm's mission was, you can imagine that it would be impossible to communicate such a set of principles to my employees. It was also impossible for me to evaluate my or the firm's performance each year to make sure the firm's operations were consistent with these values.

So, with the help of a business coach as a guide and facilitator, the entire firm met on several occasions and brainstormed portions of what our firm's mission might look like, together with a set of guiding principles for how we operated on a day-to-day basis. We put together several drafts and received input from everyone in the firm, encouraging people to speak openly and freely about their thoughts on what our firm should stand for. It wasn't until we were almost complete with the process that I realized that we were about to articulate a set of standards that could act as a guide for making difficult decisions. Just as important, we were designing how we wanted the firm to be and creating something each of us could look to and consciously make contributions to. No longer did individual employees fear how a fickle boss was going to judge them. That fear was replaced by a set of written principles they could believe in and, just as important, to which they could hold others, including me, accountable.[2]

A detailed job description, a clear evaluation process, and a mission statement (accompanied by a set of operating values) were the three legs upon which each employee's job sat. Together, they provided the guidance, motivation, and context in which a properly placed employee could thrive. However, without any one of these, the employee is left continually trying to figure out what he or she is supposed to do, why he or she is supposed to do it, and how he or she is to be compensated or rewarded for his or her actions. This kind of uncertainty can undermine anyone's confidence or motivation, or at a minimum, be a distraction. With these three pillars in place, an employee can have the stability and confidence to do the job properly, improve skills and performance, and be motivated and rewarded for efforts. Employee tenure will increase, as will productivity, and the overall atmosphere of the firm will stay positive.

2. A copy of our first mission statement and operating values is attached as Appendix 3.

7

MARKETING SECRETS

Limit Specialties and Become the Best in Those Areas

Although I did not know it at the time, I followed Steve Jobs's advice here and limited my focus to one or two areas in which to practice. Okay, it's not exactly the same, but the point is, Jobs believed that by focusing all one's resources, strengths, and energy in only a few areas, you could outthink, out-develop and out-produce your competitors. I think he proved that he was right. After all, he produced a personal computer (before there was one), a music player and a music delivery system (iPod and iTunes) that revolutionized and re-invigorated a music industry (that was dying due to piracy), revolutionized the cell phone, and created the iPad.

My professional focus on family law came as a result of my being the first attorney in Hawaii to be trained as a mediator. At the time, most attorneys thought mediation by laypersons was the unauthorized practice of law. I actually gained a reputation as an effective mediator in a pilot program between the Neighborhood Justice Center (where I had received my training) and the First Circuit Family Court in Honolulu. Once I opened my own practice, referrals flooded my business with folks who preferred an attorney who could help negotiate a settlement rather than litigate their divorce. The public got it much sooner than the lawyers.

At the time, I had been an attorney only five years and was a much better mediator than a litigator. There was even a point where I was successful in settling several seriously conflicted cases just before the trial was set to begin. There were two strangely opposite reactions to these successes: On the one hand, word got around and I received lots of positive attention from the court and fellow attorneys for these successes. On the other hand, litigation attorneys, being the competitive personalities they tend to be, concluded that my success in settlement was not so much the result of my mediation skills as it was my fear of going to trial. (A friend and colleague told me this in confidence.) As soon as this negative spin on my settlement successes was communicated to me, the settlement of any of my cases immediately halted.

This abrupt situation, compounded by my getting rusty because it had been more than two years since I had gone to trial, found me in a situation where I could not buy a settlement. All my colleagues assumed I would fold close to trial, so they all refused to settle on any reasonable terms. As part of this process, I am sure many of them over-reached their positions, which put an added burden on them at trial. As a result, I was forced to go to trial against much better, more experienced attorneys six times during the ensuing year. It scared me to death and I over-prepared for each case. I don't even recall if I made much money as I probably spent twice as much time preparing than I could charge my clients for. But that made no difference to me at the time.

I won every case that year against attorneys who had superior trial skills and many years of experience on me. Both my reputation and skills improved dramatically because of this amazing year. As a result, my business began to grow steadily. Here was another clear example of acknowledging my shortcomings and doing whatever it took to fix them. Once again, I had done the right thing—not out of good planning or strategy, but out of a choice to improve and move forward, rather than continue to wallow in the chaos of my haphazard skills and abilities.

There are two more examples indicative of why quality work is part of the secret of effective marketing of your business. The first involves my representation of a spouse of a prominent psychiatrist, who at the time was represented by an attorney that many in our community considered to be the best in town. (I was about ten years this attorney's junior.) My acceptance of the spouse as a client probably left a lot to be desired as she began making trouble soon after she retained me. It was a short marriage involving no children, so the issues should have been minimal. Nevertheless, she was out to maximize her investment in their short marriage. Fortunately, I was able to exert a significant amount of control over her and convinced her to avoid wasting money or time in litigating issues that were easily negotiable. I was apparently the first person who was able to do this. I treated the opposing party (the psychiatrist) with the respect he had earned over the years without compromising my client's position. Over the next decade, I received about a dozen quality referrals from this psychiatrist, even though he had been the opposing party. At a cocktail party some years down the road, I ran into him and thanked him for all the referrals. I asked why he did not make those referrals to his own very good attorney. His response astounded me. He said that I was the only participant in his divorce (including himself at the time) who kept a balanced perspective and who stayed focused on the resolution of his divorce as efficiently as possible. Even his own highly respected attorney only wanted to fight, and, by no mean coincidence, that would have enhanced his fees without yielding much benefit for the client. My approach not only saved the psychiatrist time and money, it allowed him to recover emotionally much more quickly than a litigated divorce would have. That recovery had assisted him in continuing his practice without much interruption. He thought this was enormous and became one of my biggest fans as a result of this experience.

The second example involved a prominent musician who came in to see me regarding a history of child support challenges. When I asked him the source of his referral to us, he said that he had asked a friend who the friend's divorce attorney was. The friend replied, "Forget my attorney, call Frank Lockwood, my ex-wife's attorney. He kicked my attorney's a--!" That is about the best endorsement one can get.

I don't know what your story is, nor do I know the extent of your training or experience. But I know that doing mediocre work will never put you in a position to grow and build the kind of firm that allows you the freedom and support that a few more attorneys, legal assistants, and administrative assistants will give you. Superior work grew my reputation in my community better than any advertising could. It also attracted the best employees because they witnessed how I operated and wanted to become part of something successful.

Many prominent prospective clients who had their choice of any of the best attorneys in town came to my door over the ensuing years. I did nothing to sell my services to them. They came into my office already convinced they would hire me because of the strength of their referral.

There is no more effective marketing strategy in the legal services industry than quality legal work and the word-of-mouth referrals that result from it.

Become a Public Servant (or Try to)

People love lawyers. I know that's contrary to conventional wisdom, and it contradicts thousands of lawyer jokes. But consider this: If you're part of a homeowners association, nonprofit organization, country club, or any board, fellow members will appreciate your input and counsel. Most of your fellow board members will be leaders in their fields and as a result will be centers of influence in areas to which you may not have much access. Your participation as an authentic, hardworking, contributing member of these boards will imprint your name in fellow board members' minds when the time comes to refer a business or family friend to a lawyer. But as repeated throughout this book, your motives in being a board member must be true. That is, your primary goal must be the betterment of the organization on whose board you serve. If your primary goal is just networking, as it is commonly referred to, and you coast as a board member, your presence may have a counterproductive effect on referrals. Who would want to hire or refer a potential client to an attorney who is not carrying their weight on the board?

A second and distinct kind of public service lies in your involvement with your local bar association. Your participation on boards, committees, and continuing education seminars brings you in contact with many other attorneys whose practices differ from yours. Hence, they are a prime source of referrals for matters within your area of expertise.

Consider that each attorney in your jurisdiction or state has his or her own following or is a center of influence in their own community. As a result, the attorney acts as a lightning rod for anyone in his or her sphere looking for legal help. Some inquiries that are directed to the attorney will be in your area of expertise. The more these attorneys know that you are a leader in your field, the more referrals you will receive from them. You may not even be the best in your field, but you can still get the referral as your bond with the other attorney may be stronger than the bond the attorney has with others in your area of practice. However, mess this case up or overbill that client, and that referral source just may dry up. As I've indicated before, quality legal work is the lubrication that keeps this and other systems discussed in this book humming along like a fine engine. If done consistently, your business will grow exponentially. Done with short cuts and shoddy work, it will freeze up, need periodic overhauls, and limp along for years without growth or real success.

Advertising Is a Waste of Time and Money

Regardless of the nature of the business, a prospective client's financial station in life is directly related to the quality of the business or service provider he or she selects. Most of these quality clients do not look for attorneys in the yellow pages, on the seat back of park benches, or in shopping carts. Just as when they want a referral to a nice restaurant, they ask their colleagues or friends for referrals. Yellow pages or park bench advertising should be reserved for personal injury attorneys, where there is no relationship between station in life and the quality of the legal work brought in. It that field of law, numbers count. Out of *x* number of personal injury claims, there will be a substantial claim and a substantial fee. It is a numbers game that does not necessarily apply to other kinds of legal work.

I tested this theory following a profitable year where an effective sales person convinced my office manager to invest some of our retained earnings into advertising. The old sales line, *If you get just one case per month from this large yellow page ad, it pays for itself. You can't lose!* was dangled in front of our noses, and we bit. What I did not realize was the resulting demand on my staff from the onslaught of phone calls from crazy, bargain-hunting, or otherwise unqualified potential clients. I had my staff log every call from potential clients to differentiate the yellow page calls from word-of-mouth referral sources.

After a few months, my office manager was ecstatic that we had received at least three phone calls per day from the yellow page ad. I then asked her to go through the list and tell me which of these calls became clients and what fees resulted from these clients. Her second report was not as enthusiastic. We had determined that the yellow page ad had done nothing more than keep my staff busy almost three hours per day, which was the time needed for the initial contact phone call, preparation and mailing of forms, temporary file set up, and follow up. It had produced no revenue from yellow page callers and cost us $3,000 per month. The insult was that I had nine more months on the contract with the phone company. Expensive lesson.

The Internet

Accurate or not, I develop my first impression of a business by looking at the Web site on the Internet. If the business doesn't have a Web site (and many small firms don't), I will pass it up for one that does. I think my approach is typical these days, especially for younger, Internet-savvy consumers. As a result, it is a must to have a Web page that presents your firm in its best light. It does not have to be expensive, and can even begin from one of those templates where you can easily post photos of all your attorneys or staff followed by a brief biography. Once your cash flow improves and you can allot a few thousand dollars to a more dynamic, informative site, you should. This kind of site can include, among other things, a list of clients (if permitted by the clients), areas of concentration, an ongoing blog of the firm's successes and news, and an FAQ section in the various procedural and substantive areas handled by the firm. Potential clients love this information. Reading it will answer many of their most common questions usually addressed to your intake coordinator or to you at the initial consultation. Consequently, you will have time to address more substantive matters during these times.

If you want your firm to appear at the top of a Google search, you need to contract with the various search engines to make this happen on a consistent basis. Depending on your area of concentration, this may or may not be cost effective. For personal injury attorneys, whose reputation and work benefit from a large network, this is most certainly the way to go. Since family law also comprises a large volume of cases in most jurisdictions, this approach also may be helpful. However, like yellow page advertising, it may cause lots of inquiries and little quality business.

The best thing about a Web presence is that it can be changed and modified easily and frequently. It can also be the beneficiary of your or your staff's unending creativity with little additional risk or cost. But a Web presence, in and of itself, will not generate new business to your firm. It will only supplement or bolster inquiries made from referrals or other, more direct sources.

8

MANAGE THE FIRM LIKE A BUSINESS

(It Is Not a Museum or an Art Gallery)

Administration

There's that word again. It's the bane of every self-important lawyer that has ever pranced around a conference table or courtroom. Proper administration is a lot like car maintenance, raising children, nurturing your marriage, or flossing your teeth: if you don't put in the time on a regular basis, something's bound to break down. Including you.

If there's anything I've tried to drive home in the previous chapters, it is that those tasks formerly relegated to the lowest levels of priority must become regularly scheduled parts of your practice if you want to move ahead, avoid repeated stresses, and increase your bottom line. I've also demonstrated that you yourself don't have to have the aptitude or personality to achieve high levels of business acumen in the running of a law firm. You simply need to acknowledge the important tasks involved in each of the preceding chapters and find, train, motivate, and reward the right employees to help you accomplish them. And, you have to schedule these tasks (for you and them) and keep to this schedule.

What follows in this chapter are additional aspects of running a law firm that don't easily fit into any of the above chapters. Mastering your skills in each of them will further bolster the effectiveness of your enterprise.

Location, Schmocation

When I had been a lawyer only a few years and finally decided that it was time to strike out on my own, I joined with a couple of equally naive and inexperienced colleagues, and embarked on probably the most wasteful and inefficient use of space and funds that I could imagine. But, we all had hopes of making lots of money which would pay for the extensive and expensive furnishings and office space for which we were about to obligate ourselves.

What a lesson.

We rented beautiful office space in a relatively new building, near the courthouse. Then, we went to one of the best office furniture stores and leased furniture for the next five years. Although I had generated an immediate following in mediation and family law through my extensive volunteer work, the financial obligation was overwhelming. I remember two distinct and repeating concerns that happened in those first few years:

1. As I was about to take a lunch break on Friday, I remember remarking that whatever money I earned after lunch that day I could keep. All my prospective earnings from Monday morning through Friday at lunch were already obligated to overhead. What a depressing thought!
2. As the end of each month approached, I had no idea where I was going to get the money to pay my only employee and the monthly lease for the space, furniture, and computer. Somehow things worked out although on several consecutive months I made it on the last day. It took a while for me to realize that all this fancy furniture and office space was robbing me of income.

I don't recommend this approach to starting or planning your business. In fact, several years later, I had changed my entire approach after a three-year stint with a large firm. This time, I went out on my own again, committing myself to the barest of obligations, by renting temporary, but nice office space in an office-sharing arrangement. Although I outgrew this arrangement within six months, I had accumulated tens of thousands of dollars in cash ready to invest in future space, furniture, and employees, without ever getting behind again in my obligations. I discovered that was the way to go.

I was now in my tenth year as an attorney. Over the next four years I watched my gross revenues double each year and my profits continue to increase even when I continued to hire new personnel. I simply made conservative investments in each of these things while making no compromises in the quality of legal work that came from the firm. I discovered that clients appreciated quality service more than fancy furniture or a prestigious address.

I discovered that choosing the best office space rarely involved location or prestige. It certainly involved convenience for clients, room for employees to work properly, and a design that was built around our needs, and not the other way around. After being downtown near the courthouse for sixteen years, I moved my office to my suburban hometown, some twelve miles from the courthouse.

My colleagues once again thought I was crazy. Clients loved it. Parking was cheap (or free), and it was better than fighting downtown traffic. My commute had gone from forty-five minutes each way to four minutes each way! And because of the growth, we moved several times, each time designing space to better meet our needs. Most landlords will offer an allowance of so much per square foot for construction costs and have a space designer on hand to assist you in the precise measurements of your space. (In addition, there are law office design books that gave us valuable insight to good design.) I gave high value to conference, reception, and copy and work areas and little value to individual offices. Large, prestigious partners' offices were a waste of money and space, space that was better allotted to workable areas. The way we ran the firm rarely allowed the clients to go anywhere other than the reception area, which needed to be pleasant and roomy, and the conference room, which accommodated a variety of functions, not the least of which was client meetings. Hence, the individual offices were really to function as workspaces rather than meeting or show spaces. The conference room also acted as a war room for major trials, as well as a party room for employees, and a deposition room during discovery. Many other small firms never ascribed importance to space for a conference room and simply didn't allow it. I found that this lack of space signaled a tight budget and cramped surroundings when it came time to do depositions or large meetings or organize a file with hundreds of exhibits.

Office Design, Furnishings, and Equipment

As alluded to above, the two most important visual aspects of your firm are the reception area and the conference room. It is in these two locations that your clients will spend most of their time. If you want to spend any money impressing clients or potential clients, this is the place to do it. The reception area provides the all-important first impression, and the conference room is where most of your client meetings will occur. If the client has never met you and is spending the first few minutes of your relationship in your reception area, you had better be aware of what it is the client is looking at and how comfortable the client is.

Early on in my practice, I bought nice leather couches for the reception area. I discovered that when several people were waiting there, two people were hesitant to sit on the same couch. Apparently sitting on a couch with a stranger impeded their sense of privacy and space. Hence, I changed to have separate and comfortable, firm-backed chairs. To further promote the sense of privacy, we also escorted one client into the conference room if we expected more than one person or party in the reception area.

There should be nothing on the floor but a new-looking carpet or hard wood, and perhaps a calming plant or two depending on your spacing. Artwork on the wall can range from historical photos to tasteful, non-offensive paintings or prints, suitably framed. As a reminder of comments in Chapter 2, this is *not* a place where you want clients to spend too much time waiting. But while they are there, you want them to be comfortable, to feel secure, and to observe that your operation appears clean, efficient, and business-like. Within this same area is where our intake coordinator (AKA receptionist) sits to greet and keep an eye on clients and potential clients. The intake coordinator should be in a relatively protected area, and her computer monitor should *never* be visible from the reception area. The networked printer/copier/scanner should be close to the intake coordinator as she uses it more than anyone in the firm, but it should also be out of sight or sound of the clients and reception area.

The conference room should contain a large table that seats at least eight people comfortably (larger if your firm has more than five attorneys). The table should have a nice finish that is cleaned daily so it is always spotless. Consider a glass-topped table. If you allow your employees to eat their lunch in the conference room, they must be scrupulous in cleaning up after themselves. If you can afford the space for a separate kitchen and avoid this potential conflict, so much the better. A kitchen allows employees to eat in and not be overly long in their lunch hour. Nevertheless, this aspect of eating in needs to be balanced by allowing your employees to leave the office midday to clear their heads and get a breath of fresh air, which may help their overall productivity.

Every employee should have his or her own computer connected to your firm's internal network, server, and the office copier/printer/scanner. Each employee should be provided with a telephone headset so talking on the phone is hands free. Employees also need strong, comfortable desk chairs as they spend many, many hours there each day. I have found desks to be the least important investment. The desk simply needs to be large enough to accommodate the computer and a work area. It is *not* a symbol of prestige or status. Your office manager, who usually handles the largest variety of tasks, should have the largest desk—perhaps even two desks and an additional working area. His or her workspace should be as large as that of any attorney or even larger. The office manager's job is the center of your firm's nervous system. You want enough room to allow organization of confidential firm files, as well as all financial and other firm records. The room should have its own lock and contain lockable file cabinets, so only you and the office manager have access. If possible, the office manager's office should be close to your office. It is not critical, but is convenient for easy and private communication between the two of you for communications regarding client, billing, personnel matters, and other important matters that seem to crop up at inopportune times.

Beyond these major kinds of furnishings for your office, I let my staff continue to design and evolve the office space to suit their needs. My only rule was that they had to justify to me how purchasing a new desk, chair, cabinet, or computer would make them more productive or help them do their job better. If they were able to do that, I usually approved the expenditure.

Technology

If your firm is properly equipped with the best software and hardware, it can compete with firms many times its size. Part of the secret to using technology well is continually training employees to use what is at their fingertips. I would estimate that the average employee uses less than half of his or her computer's software and hardware capabilities simply because the employee has not been properly trained to do so. What a waste of potential productivity! You will no doubt have varying degrees of computer skills among the employees in your firm.

There are three ways to address these technology differences so that you are not losing productivity. First, keep sending your employees to outside computer classes on frequently used software applications, such as Excel and Word. Second, have the most technologically proficient employees share their knowledge or tips with other employees and reward the trainer employees for doing so. Third, provide specific training to the employees whose job descriptions require significant technology skills, and insure that the occasional task is delegated to the most proficient person. For example, legal assistants or administrative assistants must be the best in your office in word processing because they do the lion's share of the proofreading, editing, and formatting of documents. Their training should be ongoing and advanced. If your office manager needs to write a complicated letter to a client or landlord, have them prepare a rough draft to be finished up by a more proficient word-processing person in your office. This maximizes effort and minimizes frustration. The same goes for all attorneys when preparing memoranda or briefs—rough drafts only. This practice supports the "two sets of eyes" rule regarding all documents leaving the office.

In today's world, staff proficiency in word processing, spreadsheets, e-mail, and calendaring are critical to your firm's success. To avoid potentially repetitive tasks, keep electronic contact managers (which should include e-mail addresses) updated daily and use e-mail groups. Your firm's software for timekeeping and billing, calendaring, and contacts should automatically sync and update every day to every computer on your system. In fact, each attorney should have a smartphone that includes synced calendar and e-mail so he or she can make appointments or schedule court dates when outside the office without creating conflicts. Today's cloud technology allows this with ease. IPads that can communicate or transmit documents through cell phone lines are also extremely useful for working away from the office. They can be used for video conferencing, retrieving forgotten documents, or even viewing another location while in a deposition or in court. The world can be viewed at your fingertips for little cost on a clear, lightweight screen.

Delegating tasks to staff in your firm by e-mail is the very best way to create, track, and follow to-do lists. With e-mail, there is less ambiguity about what is involved in the task (or at least, there's an opportunity to clarify the assignment). It is clear when the assignment is given and when it is due. It cannot fall between the cracks as it is always in the list of e-mails regardless of how they are sorted, so that it never gets lost until completed.

I used Macintosh computers from the time they were introduced until the present day. I discovered that because of this, I had two basic advantages over PC users: One, my staff and I learned how to use the computers faster and in more ways than PC users, and therefore we could accomplish more. Two, the computers crashed less, or put another way, had less maintenance or downtime and costs devoted to maintenance. As a result, my staff could create, organize, and move information faster than our competitors. And, as indicated above, our billing system could turn billable hours into cash flow better than my competitors' systems. The only caveat was that we had challenges for a few years with time-and-billing programs not supported by the Mac. This was easily solved when the Mac was able to run Windows software flawlessly, in effect giving my staff and me two computers in one. Today, with smartphones that can automatically sync with as many computers or mobile devices as you have, the Apple system is more evolved and more integrated than those in the PC world.

I also avoided thousands of dollars in storage costs by having all my files that were over one year old scanned, burned onto CDs, and stored on a backup server. Once high-speed scanners were introduced (at last count, seventy pages per minute), this transition to a digital storage system became quick and easy, and it saved us from the expense of extra evening or weekend workers to accomplish this work. As a result, we never had to rent outside, inconvenient storage space that added to our overhead or deal with logistics headaches when we needed to retrieve or research old files.

A seamless backup system is integral to the safety of your documents as well as your time-and-billing records. These systems can accomplish daily incremental backups of all new information produced on your system and create full, global backups weekly. It is advisable to have weekly backups stored off site for the purposes of security and safety, and to test these backup media periodically to make sure the information can actually be retrieved.

Finally, and as indicated in Chapter 1, information flow of hundreds of important documents or correspondence can be transmitted to every person in the firm who needs to be aware of the documents without ever losing a document or wasting time. And through e-mail, these documents can be retrieved and sorted by client or date if necessary. In addition, documents or correspondence can be stored separately in the client's digital and paper file for added safety and redundancy. The original documents rarely travel from the intake coordinator to anywhere other than the paper file, further insuring close tracking of important papers.

Insurance

Your office manager should be tasked with the responsibility of reviewing all your insurance coverage annually to make sure you are getting the most bang for your buck, as well as if the firm has grown, determining whether increases in liability or casualty coverage might be warranted. Your local bar association can usually help because its staff may have reviewed or approved many insurers used by firms in your jurisdiction. In addition, check with other colleagues' firms in the area to find out who insures them, what the costs are, and the general feedback on the insurers. You will need to review your policies for the business, including property and casualty, and make decisions about whether you want to partially self-insure by increasing your deductibles and lowering your premiums as a result.

Errors-and-omissions (malpractice) insurance is required in most jurisdictions. Even if it is not required in your jurisdiction, it is worth having. Most small law firms that specialize in a few areas rarely get malpractice claims filed against them. As a result, a high deductible will lower your premiums appreciably while insuring you against catastrophic claims. This is where you can derive the most peace of mind.

For the major partners in the firm, you may also want to consider key-man life insurance with the firm as a beneficiary because it is one way to insure cash flow. You might also want additional life insurance with remaining partners as direct beneficiaries to help insure against the loss of a partner's earning power. Depending on the age and health of the partners, term policies for twenty years can be relatively economical.

Create an Asset

After about twenty-five years of practicing law, I began to wonder what the world was like outside the practice, both physically (as in the Great Wall of China or the Grand Canyon) and mentally, as in seeing how folks who weren't in court all the time or working out of a cube called an office lived. I slowly began to develop an exit strategy that would allow me to retire way before the normal retirement period—my sixties—or, as is frequently the case with lawyers—my seventies. You may not be thinking about retirement, but the end result is something you absolutely should be aware of.

That is, have you created value in your firm that is recognizable in the marketplace? Or, when the time comes to close your doors, is it a worthless asset with no market value? Being business oriented most of my career, I was bothered that solo practitioners' businesses, whether they be chiropractors or lawyers, had virtually no market value beyond their own so-called goodwill. As a result, their businesses were worth very little without the continued presence of that practitioner. At the same time, another more mundane business, whether a cleaners or fast-food franchise, could have enormous value beyond its identity with the owner. This just didn't seem right.

It became clear over the years that my business would not be worth much beyond my goodwill unless I either stayed around on a part-time basis with my name still on the door, or I built the firm so that my personal efforts were a small portion of the firm's revenue production.

I have two colleagues whose participation in their practices has been cut back to the point of allowing them to be gone half the year or to travel extensively while still maintaining a presence within the firm. The three of us transitioned out of full-time law practice in three completely different ways. All were valid approaches and all are working well for the time being.

1. Owner one, let's call him Ted, specialized in trust litigation and had a fine reputation among estate planning and many other types of attorneys. He and his wife loved to travel and concocted a plan to go RVing for six months each year. Ted was able to find an associate that apprenticed with him for a couple of years to develop his expertise in the same area. When the time came for Ted and his wife to depart in their luxury motor coach, the apprentice took over management of the day-to-day practice and had full responsibility for managing all costs related to running the firm, such as rent, employee wages, insurance, and so on. Ted's name stayed on the door and he stayed in contact with his apprentice through mobile Internet access wherever he was. Ted's wife prepared billing and handled other administrative functions from her laptop inside the motor home. Ted worked about ten to twenty hours per week, depending on demand, for the six-month period when he and his wife traveled. His billings were added to his apprentice's billing on the monthly bills sent to clients. He and his apprentice negotiated mutually agreeable terms regarding dividing the revenue. After six months of traveling across the United States, Ted and his wife return home and Ted occupies the spare office at the firm. He returns to full-time practice after seeing the world and working at a very relaxed pace. Ted has practiced the routine of six months off and six months on successfully for three years.
2. The second owner, let's call him Chad, owned a much larger family law firm. Years before his transition, he had sold a minority interest in the practice to his partner. This sale created an asset for Chad that could be used for retirement, investment, or any other purpose. The point is that just the sale of an interest in the firm created an asset for Chad. After several years of a successful partnership, Chad's partner purchased the remaining interest in the firm, with the firm's name not changing for either change in ownership interest.

Chad's "partner" is now the sole owner of the firm and managing partner as well. Chad still works in the firm devoting most of his working hours to mediation—the less paper- and court-intensive cases—where his skills are best applied. He has no remaining personal financial stake or worries associated with the firm, and he gets paid for the work he performs at a rate that benefits both him and his partner. It is a perfect marriage between the partners.

3. The third scenario was the one I used. It involved replacing myself with a skilled trial lawyer and manager who would some day take over management of the firm and buy me out completely. The fundamentals of this process involved finding the right person who could carry out the high level of quality delivery of legal services I established for the firm. It also involved evolving the firm to the point where my personal legal work accounts for a minority of the firm's income. This is done for two reasons: First, my ultimate withdrawal will not harm the firm's revenue, and second, because the partner purchasing my interest will have the incentive of eliminating my large salary and benefits from the firm's books. The extra cash flow generated from the termination of my salary and benefits can be used to finance the buyout or used as part of the buyout if complete financing is not available for a cash sale.

The choice of scenario depends on your future plans and personal goals. If you are planning on staying in the area and living a lifestyle similar to the one you had before the transition (except that you may take more vacations or travel more), then either of the first two scenarios may be the choice for you. You and your purchasing partner would have to have a sound, trusting relationship that allows you the flexibility to come and go with some amount of discretion and planning on your part. And, you would need a desire to continue to practice your craft, without the financial or management responsibilities or time pressures of full-time practice or ownership. If you are planning on relocating to a different part of the world or want to devote a substantial amount of your time to other pursuits, like I did, then a more complete buyout like the one described above is more appropriate.

Most of these buyouts involve some type of objective business valuation and flexibility on the part of the buyer and the seller. It would behoove you to learn the fundamentals of business valuation as you start down this road, or get an informal or preliminary valuation done and have the person performing the valuation coach you on how to increase your firm's value for purposes of future sale.

9

KNOW YOUR NUMBERS

This is not Rocket Science or Voodoo Economics. It's Accounting

In the early days of owning my law firm, I would occasionally be sitting at a seminar or luncheon and have little or no interest in what was going on. I would begin to wonder why I was working so hard and not making nearly as much money as I should be. I would jot down a list of my billable employees (at the beginning there were only three or four, including myself). Next to this column, I would list another column of each of our respective billing rates. In a third column, I would write a conservative number of hours each day that I could reasonably expect each of us to bill. The fourth column would be the total of multiplying columns two and three to get an amount of income I could reasonably expect from each employee's efforts. I would total the dollar amount in the fourth column to find out how much money I could reasonably expect to bring in each day, and then I would multiply this daily number by 21 days per month to find out how much money I could reasonably expect to bring in that month. Under that number, I would write the number representing my average monthly nut (more formally referred to as my monthly overhead).

This simple handwritten spreadsheet would look something like this:

Frank	$250.00/hr	X 6 hrs/day	$1,500
Jennifer	$150.00	6	$900
Kalani	$90.00	6	$540
Eileen	$90.00	6	$540
			$3,480
			21 days/mo
	Potential monthly income		$73,080
	Ave monthly overhead		$35,000
	Potential monthly profit		$38,080

If the monthly overhead number was smaller that the billing total, I would be looking at my monthly profit, right? Well, if that was so, why wasn't I making the profit indicated above each and every month so I could use some of that money for a lease on a new BMW?

The answers to these and many other questions about numbers are in this chapter. The only thing I can't answer is why you are not driving a BMW. (Or worse, why you are driving one and struggling to make the monthly payments on it.)

What Is Your Effective Billing Rate (EBR) and Why Is It Useful?

All attorneys know what their billing rate is, but few have ever bothered to find out what their *effective billing rate* (EBR) is. If, for example, your billing rate is $250 per hour and you bill 100 hours that month, you have billed $25,000 for that month's work. If however, based upon those billings, you collect say 75% of your billings, or $18,750, and the remainder goes into the accounts receivable column (AR), your EBR for that month is $187.50 per hour ($18,750 divided by 100 hours), not the $250 per hour you enjoy shocking your non-lawyer friends with at cocktail parties. This number is useful in a variety of circumstances to assist you in understanding how your business works and how you create (or fail to create) positive cash flow. It is also one of many factors in evaluating performance of yourself and your employees.

Let's now apply your EBR (using the same collection ratio of 75% to all of your billing employees) to the simple spreadsheet above and see perhaps a more realistic number for your potential profit each month:

Frank	$187.50	6	$1,125
Jennifer	$112.50	6	$675
Kalani	$67.50	6	$405
Eileen	$67.50	6	$405
			$2,610
			21
	Potential monthly income		$54,810
	Ave monthly overhead		$35,000
	Potential monthly profit		$19,810

Wait a minute! You still don't see that balance added to your bank account each month. Oh yeah, taxes. Let's subtract state and federal taxes from that bottom line to see a more realistic number:

Frank	$187.50	6	$1,125
Jennifer	$112.50	6	$675
Kalani	$67.50	6	$405
Eileen	$67.50	6	$405
			$2,610
			21
	Potential monthly income		$54,810
	Ave monthly overhead		$35,000
	Potential monthly profit		$19,810
	State & Federal taxes of 40%		-$7,924
	After tax monthly profit		$11,886

Now this bottom line number seemed more in line with my experience. At least I knew that I could still maintain positive cash flow and meet my obligations with this conservative analysis of my firm's monthly revenue-producing potential, *if*

- the client selection process was done properly, and

- my office manager or assistant kept an eye on the trust account balances, and
- phone calls were made monthly to those clients who failed to timely replenish their trust account balances.

If these parts of the system were followed, I could expect to deposit no less than 50% of the billings, but more reasonably 60% to 75% of the firm's monthly billings into my business bank account *on the day that the invoices are e-mailed to clients*. Within two weeks of the invoices going out, additional revenue from client payments should reasonably bring the total current month's receipts to 75% of the previous month's billing.

What happened to the remaining 25% of the billings? Those numbers went into the accounts receivable totals in your billing program. How those are addressed will determine whether you run a moderately profitable firm or a very profitable firm. (See Chapter 4 to learn the process of moving those numbers back into your monthly income statement.)

Understanding and Using Your Financial Statements

There are three things, in general, that you need to know about using your financial statements. (By financial statements, I specifically mean your profit-and-loss statement, balance sheet, and cash-flow statement.)

1. How are they set up?
2. How do they work together?
3. What do they tell you?

One of the biggest failings of setting up your chart of accounts is adopting the one in QuickBooks that you think is proper without consulting with a CPA. Don't be intimidated by the phrase *chart of accounts*. It is just the accountant's term for the categories you assign to your income, expenses, assets, and debts. For example, common expense categories are rent, salaries, insurance, and so on. Common asset categories are bank account balances, office equipment, clients' trust accounts, and leasehold improvements.

Make sure you use a CPA who is familiar with law firm practice. The accountant will set up a chart of accounts designed for a service business and will customize these accounts to make them useful for your analyses. Make sure that the accounts are broken down enough to allow you to track them month to month, and note any variations. Then you can inquire whether these variations are reasonable or not.

For tax purposes, you probably will set up your financial statements on the cash-basis method of accounting. This simply means that you record exactly what leaves your checking account and what gets deposited into it each month. It also means that you only pay taxes on income actually received. For small- to medium-sized law firms, this makes sense since you want to show the connection between income for a month and the expenses incurred to create that income.

However, the cash-basis method (which is really no more than balancing your checkbook) has marginal usefulness when it comes to analyzing the real costs of running your firm, especially on a long-term basis. Many accountants will recommend that you keep your books on an accrual basis, so you can better analyze the true average cost of running the business and predict and spread income and costs out over the years rather than be hit with an unplanned expenditure, like an annual insurance premium or a tax bill. Both methods have their uses as long as you understand that the cash-basis method is a short-term view of your business and the accrual method is a longer-term view. Both are accurate views of the financial health of your firm, but only for the time period indicated.

For example, if you pay an annual premium of $5,000 for errors-and-omissions insurance, the monthly profit of the month in which you pay it will drop $5,000 compared to the monthly profit in other months of the year. Looking long term, however, the average monthly cost of that insurance premium is really only $417 per month. The accrual method allows you to set aside this sum each month so you are not surprised when the insurance premium is paid. The cash method merely informs you that the payment has been made.

In either case, you will want to have your administrative person create a cash-flow statement to show you *exactly* where the money came from and went to each month. It is this cash-flow statement that will help you make sure your business runs smoothly, so that things like rent and salaries are paid on time. It will also quickly (1) inform you when your expenditures exceed your income, (2) indicate how often this happens, and (3) allow you to make changes in your operation to prevent this from happening often.

The most useful aspect of having your monthly accounting done in-house is having immediate access to up-to-the-minute numbers when you want them. Today we live in the world of QuickBooks accounting software, making it easy for an office manager who is moderately trained in bookkeeping to save you time and money by producing both monthly profit-and-loss statements (P&L), as well as a balance sheet. The office manager can also produce valuable cash-flow projections as well.

If you have a firm of three to five attorneys, a few legal assistants, and various administrative staff, and you are sending your accounting functions to an outside bookkeeping firm, you are wasting your money and placing another layer of administration between that information and yourself. Your money is much better spent on training a staff member to keep track of the books and having those books reviewed by your outside accountant, who can make adjustments periodically to insure accuracy and maximize your deductions. If you use an outside bookkeeper you are waiting much too long to find out the status of your cash flow and profit. It will be difficult to get that up-to-the-minute information regarding your firm's numbers. In fact, QuickBooks allows you to tap into the server where the firm's financial files are kept (in password-protected files) and produce these reports at 11:00 P.M. from home if you can't sleep. The reports you want can be preformatted ahead of time by your accountant, so that all you need to do is set date parameters and push a button.

The most basic function of the monthly profit-and-loss statement is to determine how much it costs to operate your firm—your monthly nut, as it is frequently called. When comparing several months' statements, you can note variations in expenditures such as insurance payments or office supplies and find out the reason for these variations. In QuickBooks, you can do this instantly by simply double-clicking on the individual expense in the report, and up pops a detailed report showing every transaction that is part of this expense. You cannot do this if your only interaction with your financial statements is holding a piece of paper in your hand.

You will also gain perspective of where the majority of expenses are concentrated (such as salaries or office rent), so that you can focus on expanding areas that produce more benefit than they cost, or trim areas of expense that produce little or no financial benefit. For example, it amazed me to realize that the cost of adding an additional administrative employee was the same as adding an additional 1,000 square feet of office space. It is valuable to know these ratios and comparisons when trying to make decisions of where the points of pressure are to expand, and what the benefits are of comparative expansion in different areas.

Your balance sheet, while having only marginal usefulness in accounting for the assets of a small law firm, provides a real pattern of the health of your business when tracking your asset-to-debt ratios. Simply put, if the asset-to-debt ratio is increasing each month, your business is growing. If this ratio decreases each month, your business is shrinking. Your banker will look at this ratio, both the ratio itself as well as its pattern, when deciding if you are a low risk for a line of credit, as well as what line of credit you can support.

Business owners are often confused about why their profit for the year doesn't show up in their bank account. "If I made so much money, why isn't there any left in my account?" This is where the cash-flow report comes in handy. It shows you where your money *really* went. The after-tax spreadsheet example earlier in this chapter showed that the month's net profit was $11,886. Why didn't this amount end up in the bank account? The cash-flow report might show you that $4,000 was used to pay back the line of credit draws or to purchase a computer that is not considered an expense that would show up on the profit-and-loss statement. Comparing cash-flow reports from month to month will show you where your cash really went.

Cash-Flow Heaven

Can I Afford It?

Using your financial statements for planning purposes will enable you to determine the real cost of expanding your office space or adding new employees to your payroll (the costs of additional Social Security and Medicare payments, office space, employee benefits, bonuses, incentives, additional administrative support, and paid vacations) before adding that employee, instead of being shocked when you experience that your cost for the employee runs you about 133% of that employee's base salary.

Once you have a handle on your newly found cash-flow knowledge, you are ready to make informed decisions on new hires or capital investments in your firm (such as new computers, furniture, or enlarged office space). If, for example, you can generate enough net cash-flow over a three-month period to cover the added monthly expenses of a new hire, and it takes six months to get a legal assistant or new attorney generating enough revenue to cover all the related expenses, you have just created options for when and how to finance this new hire. You can wait nine months to make this new hire so that you don't have to borrow money to meet the new, immediate added expenses, or you can simply finance the hire through your firm's line of credit.

Typically, the awareness of your firm's staffing needs is much more obvious and immediate than your knowledge of whether you can afford to meet those needs in a timely manner. As a result, the most practical solution to meeting staffing needs if and when they arise is having an accessible line of credit. When hiring an experienced lawyer or legal assistant who can be productive from day one, your additional cash flow needs will be much smaller. In either case, once the hire begins producing revenue above and beyond his or her own costs to the firm, you can methodically and intentionally pay back the line of credit draws that you made to accommodate that new hire.

All of this can be planned in advance. Variations on the accuracy of this plan will occur as a result of the efficiency and effectiveness of all the other components that make up this entire ecosystem. If you experienced no bumps in your client selection in the previous few months, and your staff carries out their responsibilities in the billing-and-collection system described previously, all will work out according to schedule. The larger the client base, the more likely this will happen with machine-like efficiency. You can drastically reduce the number and severity of cash flow challenges when using this system. You do not have to be an accountant to know the numbers of your business. It's simple math, and your accountant can help you overcome fear of financial statements. Once you begin reviewing your monthly income and expenses, and the inflow and outflow of your cash, you will begin to run your law firm like a business.

10

YOU NEED PROFESSIONAL HELP

A CPA Is Like Gold

Neither you nor your bookkeeper has the expertise needed to discern the deeper meaning and implications of every aspect of your financial statements. Nor do you have the time to develop that expertise that a good CPA has taken years of education and experience to hone.

Use your CPA to review and revise (as needed) your P&L and balance sheets each month or each quarter. The one or two hours the CPA spends with your bookkeeper will be paid back to you in lack of heartburn and peace of mind because your statements are accurate and have been coded or categorized properly. It is also good practice to have an independent, outside expert review all your transactions to avoid any potential internal monkey business.

As indicated in the previous chapter, your CPA also will be able to assist you in customizing your profit-and-loss statements to examine specific areas or profit centers that you may not otherwise be able to analyze. Customized statements can help you draw conclusions about whether various departments or areas of your firm are run efficiently or could be run more efficiently. Your CPA can point out potential areas of waste or suggest areas of improvement with different staffing arrangements or allocation of resources.

You want your CPA to advise you on estimated quarterly tax payments so that you're not hit with a big bill at tax time. How you choose to approach this is up to you. You may want to spread out the pain to be consistent with your cash flow, or you may want to minimize your payments to increase your cash flow throughout the year and finance the difference at tax time. My preference is to spread the pain so that my view of my cash flow is consistent and predictable. I don't like big surprises or spending money that is not really mine. Living beyond the firm's needs is not the way to produce long-term wealth.

The other point of view is that you are giving the IRS money that does nothing for you over a period of a year. It brings you no return on your investment; it's not like using the money for a new copy machine or new computers put into use early to assist your staff in becoming more productive. I prefer to view estimated tax payments as a reserve fund that provides me a financial cushion. Then, if I need additional cash flow, I can borrow from the line of credit for short periods of time. These different options and their consequences should be discussed thoroughly with your CPA.

In the final quarter of your fiscal year, your CPA can assist you in planning for bonuses and capital expenditures that can be written off completely as expenses or in finding ways to accelerate your depreciation, all of which are strategies to lower your taxes. You can, for example, pay bonuses, purchase equipment, make contributions to a 401(k) or other retirement plan, on or before December 31 (if you're on a calendar year), and collect fees on January 1 for December work of the previous year, thereby maximizing your expenses for this year (and, as a result, lowering your taxes), and deferring tax liability for the new income for twelve months. You can save thousands of dollars by timing these transactions to occur only one day apart. These transactions can be accomplished whether you have the cash flow or not to support them since you have your credit line. Financing will only be for one day, thereby costing you virtually nothing.

All of these possibilities, and other creative and legal transactions should be discussed at least a month before you plan to implement them. The planning should include your bookkeeper, in confidence, to insure you won't create any real cash flow challenges at an inopportune time.

Human Resources Resources

There are two areas where you will probably need assistance in order to avoid running afoul of employment laws and minimize employee rules and confusion: (1) the posting of and adherence to federal and state employment laws, and (2) the creation of a consistent, well thought-out employee manual.

There are at least three major resources you can turn to for help in addressing these needs. A business trade organization such as an Employer's Council or Chamber of Commerce is one. These organizations exist in part to support small business in the increasingly complicated area of employment law and regulations. They provide literature and required posters for your office and seminars to assist you or your human resources person in complying with the law. In addition to these organizations, there is an enormous amount of information on the Internet that is helpful if you don't have a business trade organization in your immediate area. For example, the U.S. Department of Labor (http://www.dol.gov/elaws/) has a very user-friendly site for employees and employers alike. It is a huge site and includes different ways of accessing information or help you may need.

The U.S. Small Business Administration site (http://www.sba.gov/content/employment-and-labor-law) offers state-specific searches and help, and it also lists many offices in each state if you want to get help in a face-to-face meeting.

My firm joined the employer's council in my area, which cost significantly more than the chamber of commerce, but it supplied formidable help for employers in my state. Such help included focused seminars for my HR person, forms and posters that complied with federal and state regulations, and ready guidance when we needed it. In addition, I simply became a client of the largest law firm in the state whose clientele included businesses on the management side of labor disputes. I developed a relationship with one of the lawyers there who would answer all my inquiries promptly no matter how small. This relationship saved time when employment challenges arose and helped me not make those challenges worse when they occurred. What's more, the advice was often available within the same day. The law firm also supplied me with a template, both hard copy and digital, for an employee manual. Going through the template and filling in the blanks, and making decisions on matters such as sick or maternity leave, vacations or vacation pay, dress code, and so on, was an invaluable experience. It helped me think through many potential problems and nip most of them in the bud before they happened.

Your Banker Is Your Friend

As alluded to in several chapters earlier, a line of credit (LOC) with your local bank is an invaluable resource. The size of the line can vary but should be no less than one-and-a-half times your monthly overhead. Banks typically require annual renewal, complete with submission of current financial statements. Banks also compete for your business, so it is worth shopping around. The variety of approaches, costs, and requirements will astound you. The same goes for setting up a merchant account for taking credit cards. Comparing systems and fees is critical in this area. A difference of half a percent can cost or save you tens of thousands of dollars over a period of a year for doing nothing more than shopping smart.

Securing a line of credit is only half the challenge. Using it properly is the other half. The line of credit should only be used for short-term cash flow challenges that might occur between billing cycles. It should then be paid down or off, even if for only a few days. Remember, the banks charge you interest on the average daily balance on your LOC. Hence, if you can pay down the balance, your interest charge is reduced. Better yet, pay it off for even one day, and your average daily balance has just been cut in half for that period.

The problem with many small firms who use a LOC is that they use it as an overdraft account and never seem to pay it off. Doing this is no different that carrying a balance on your credit card. In the long run, you end up paying more for the goods and services you purchase. Similarly, in business, you end up increasing your monthly overhead, and that is counterproductive. So this bears repeating: The LOC is for smoothing out short-term cash flow challenges. It is not designed for a firm that lives beyond its means. Every LOC balance should be explainable in short terms and should have a plan supporting its extinction on a short-term basis.

Typically, the inability of your firm frequently to pay off its LOC is a symptom of poor billing-and-collection practices (see Chapter 4), or on a deeper level, poor client selection practices (see Chapter 2). A brief analysis of these methods can mitigate this problem in your firm and, depending on its level, it can be extinguished within a few months.

Get Your Own Lawyer

Lawyers, like doctors, seem to be chronic violators of their own advice. They seem to think they can represent themselves is a variety of situations—in areas where they have no business practicing. Small firm or sole practitioners are infamous for either taking on cases in which they have no expertise or guidance, or worse, representing themselves in areas where a specialist can do a better, more efficient job. Areas such as workers' compensation, various employee challenges including wrongful termination, and landlord-tenant matters, especially the negotiation of leases, are best left to the experts. We advise our clients to hire a specialist in areas they need. We just need to abide by our own advice.

Just make sure you hire the right attorney for the right matter. If you're negotiating terms of a lease, you may prefer a commercial real estate attorney to advise you on the desirable or undesirable terms presented to you in your lease. You may, however, want to negotiate those terms yourself if you have negotiation expertise. If not, you may want to hire someone who is more comfortable in this area. Your productivity in the areas you are good at will usually more than balance out the fees you need to pay. That is another way of saying that you may be losing valuable billing opportunities because you are ignoring work that is waiting for you, so you can attend to a problem in which you are an amateur. Many times your colleagues will comp your fees in exchange for your reciprocity at a later time.

What Are You Good at?

Part of the secret of running an efficient law firm is distinguishing between the things you are good at and the things you are not so good at. Your goal, then, is to find or train someone else to handle those things you are not good at.

This is not an easy task for a person driven by ego as many lawyers are. It requires a calm assessment that while you may be good at legal analysis, or even good at interpersonal communication, you may be awful at hiring (as I was), or organization. If you are a good family lawyer and have all the work you can handle, you have no business addressing other types of problems or challenges in your firm. The revenue created by your billable time should be more than enough to compensate you for the cost of these other challenges. Your uninterrupted time and focus on the work you are paid to do goes a long way to support the good service and quality you strive for.

Being a jack-of-all-trades will only dilute your effectiveness and break the concentration needed to develop good strategies or effective case preparation. You will float between a shallow approach to the practice of law and keeping your head above water financially. Hence, a major focus of this book is to convince you to delegate to specialists in different areas who can provide the support you need to practice law as best as you can. Every time you try to be something you're not, you dilute that effectiveness.

11

LAW FIRM ECOSYSTEM

Everything Is Connected to Everything Else

Evolution of the Practice of Law

In the process of writing each chapter, I began to discover that what at first glance appeared to be the treatment of separate and distinct areas of running and operating a law firm were really more like the delicately balanced, minute parts of an ecosystem, if you will. Any failure of a small part of one can pervade the entire system and cause any number of failures in the system as a whole. For example, if too much focus is put on the bottom line, compromises will be made in quality and efficiency of work, salaries may not be in alignment with the quality of work done, employees may experience frequent or constant stress, and clients may be unhappy with the experience. It was then that I began to realize why many lawyers leave the practice each year, why many people are unhappy with their experiences with lawyers, and why the billable hour is being challenged as the best way to charge clients for legal services.

Conversely, I found that success in human resources, for example, had a positive impact on employee retention. This, in turn, had a positive impact on motivating employees and reducing stress, resulting in the overall improvement in quality of work these employees produced.

And so it went. I began to realize that the vicious circle of tension and stress I had previously felt could be reversed. Instead of feeling like I was balancing three plates on three sticks, where my focus on one threatened my focus on the other two, I began to see a different approach, one in which refinement and efficiency in one area supported the vitality and sustainability of the others. For example, a good billing system supported good cash flow. Good cash flow supported quality hiring and higher pay for better employees, and better employees supported higher quality of work product. Higher quality of work product brought better clients.

You get the picture.

I believed (and had experienced) that if things were done right, you, the small law firm owner or solo practitioner, could have it all: financial success, lower-than-normal stress, and a balanced life. The demands of legal work, admin, and home were not in competition with each other at all. Rather, they were all part of a finely tuned ecosystem where each part consisted of many small components. If each component were in alignment with the others, it could and would support a balanced, healthy, and successful lifestyle.

The fully integrated ecosystem of any organization is critical to its long-term success. Whether the organization is a baseball team, a large corporation, a political party, or a nation, its ecosystem is a fragile and co-dependent mixture of that organization's beliefs and values and the behavior of its members or citizens. It takes a long time to develop a truly sound, positive ecosystem and only moments to destroy it.

A law firm is no different. Of the many factors that go into creating or maintaining a law firm ecosystem, the incentives provided to its employees is paramount. If the incentive of the employee is billing, everything an employee does, whether that employee is an attorney or legal assistant, will be viewed and influenced through the billing lens. If the focus is on looking good, the employees will act and dress to achieve this goal. Unfortunately, very few of these types of incentives are either client centered or quality centered. That is, they don't necessarily result in producing better legal work.

A complicating factor is confusion by the employees when written or stated goals or incentives are not followed by the partners or owners of the firm. The firm may stand for one set of principles or mission, but the partners or owners seem to behave with their own set of rules, feeling exempt because of their position. This kind of hypocrisy merely widens the gap between the staff, associates, and the owners of the firm. Employees will not confide in partners about their concerns for fear of not fitting with a confusing mission. Or worse, the employee will fake some form of fearlessness or false bravado that he or she feels is expected by the partners. Real problems don't get addressed until they are in crisis mode. Long-term planning suffers as it rarely identifies systemic problems in a culture of fear.

For example, many law firms require each timekeeper (lawyer or legal assistant) to bill eight hours per day—1,800 to 2,000 hours per year. Others pay their lawyers a base salary and add to that salary additional income based upon bringing in revenue of more than a certain dollar amount per month. Let's examine where the incentives drive these employees.

First, the lawyer or legal assistant is immediately faced with a dilemma of meeting a court or case deadline, while, at the same time, punished financially for being efficient. The stress caused by these apparently conflicting goals can be staggering. The temptation to pad bills can be overwhelming when considering the personal goals and benefits to lawyer's or legal assistant's families. Each and every decision about how to approach each step of a case will be influenced by the lawyer's judgment about how such a decision will affect his or her personal financial success or welfare. This is a ridiculous way to practice law. Unfortunately, it is the status quo throughout the profession.

In addition to overbilling, the lawyer may be tempted to litigate issues that should be settled for fear that settling might result in lower legal fees in the case. This kind of behavior is often rationalized as zealous advocacy for the client—not showing any weakness in the attorney's commitment to the client's cause. The phrase *zealous advocacy* used to appear in the attorney's ethical code until the profession finally realized that most lawyers misunderstood and abused its meaning. Attorneys actually thought it meant that they were ethically bound to act like zealots! Although such behavior may not be to the client's benefit, it is most certainly perceived as being to the benefit of the lawyer's short-term finances or career. The attorney whose compensation is directly tied to monthly revenue numbers will not seek the help of others in the firm for fear of giving away billable time to his or her competitors in the firm. He will hoard his work. The many benefits of teamwork, such as creativity and efficiency, are lost to the client and the case under this type of compensation system.

At one time in my career, I had either a trial or a motion against several attorneys of one law firm whose compensation was directly tied to their monthly revenue numbers. Over a period of approximately two years, we litigated eighteen different cases. My clients prevailed on all eighteen motions or trials. During this period, I once asked one of their chief litigators whether it bothered him to lose at trial or to represent a client with a legally unsupportable position. He said, "Not at all!" This was because this attorney defined his success the same way his employer defined it: money. It had nothing to do with the quality of his legal work, or a sound, cost–effective analysis of deciding which cases to settle and which to litigate. It was a very simple explanation as to why this firm consistently lost its cases against my firm.

I, on the other hand, disliked losing so much that I only took cases to trial or court that I was pretty sure were winners. When I was not sure that a position my client wanted to take to court was a winning one, I honestly and frankly told the client this. I even estimated the chances of success and the cost of losing. This prompted many clients to settle an issue or entire case. They appreciated that I was not rolling the dice with their money. I was allowing them to make a decision based upon an honest assessment of the strengths and weaknesses of their case. This, I believed, was what the client hired me to do.

This built a strong reputation for our firm and signaled to other attorneys that if we were going to trial, we were not bluffing. I also ended up with many happy clients, a rarity in family law practice.

If a lawyer's compensation and rewards were based upon the quality of his work, each decision on how to approach a case would involve a much simpler, client-centered approach, and the lawyer would not be placed in an obvious conflict-of-interest position with his client, where minimizing fees may be in the client's best interests and maximizing fees may be in the lawyer's career interests. This is an incompatible set of incentives on which to base one's professional approach to the practice of law.

To achieve the desired ecosystem of a law firm, one must, as Stephen Covey stated in his book, *The Seven Habits of Highly Successful People,* start with the end in mind. All incentives and all decisions about how to design and assemble the components of a law firm must be judged by the desired end. Although the variables are many and can seem confusing and even contradictory at times, taken one at a time, they can be managed to create a viable and enduring law firm ecosystem with a clear and simple end of delivering high quality legal services. If the end you seek is the delivery of high quality legal work, then it becomes easier to look back on the various systems you have set up to determine whether they support or sabotage this end.

It all starts with the senior partner or owner. Once created, the clearly stated goal of delivering high quality legal services, further expounded by your mission statement and set of operating values, provides a guideline to all members of the firm.

My personal and professional belief is that the delivery of high quality legal services should be the preeminent goal of any law firm. Once every decision in hiring, employee training, and incentives is made with this goal in mind, every other desirable goal of its owners and members will be achieved as a by-product of this goal.

Many owners of firms believe that a law firm ecosystem can be achieved through decorating, office location, or even by the character of its clients. This is the tail wagging the dog. It is as if you have decided to become a golfer and first gone out and bought the best clubs, best gear, and joined the best country club before you ever took a golf lesson. That is backwards.

A law firm ecosystem is a funny thing. It has many moving parts. After thirty years of participating in my own and several other firms, I believe a firm's character is really the sum of its parts. Different from the billing goal in most law firms and certainly different from the large firm I worked for early in my career, the billing goal that I set was six billable hours per day per timekeeper rather than the standard eight. Although timekeepers were in the office at least eight hours per day, what did they do with the extra two hours per day? Well, that was up to them. They could go to the gym at or before lunch. They could visit on the phone, or do Facebook or personal e-mail with their family or friends.

They could also spend a little extra time keeping track of their time. Whatever they did, they could not complain that their billable hours were difficult to attain. Nor would they be tempted to pad their timekeeping. Among many of the factors used to evaluate their performance annually, timekeeping was only one. And since I knew my numbers (see Chapter 9), six hours billed by each billing person in the law firm had the potential to create plenty of profit for me, the owner.

If an employee exceeded the timekeeping minimum, they were graded higher in their evaluation in that area. However, there were many areas in which employees, especially attorneys and legal assistants, were evaluated. What I did *not* want was to have timekeeping be the major factor in determining my employees' financial rewards.

Conclusion

The truth of the matter is, mastery of *any one* of the above systems described in each of the above chapters will significantly improve the operation of your law firm. You don't need to feel that you have to master them all to start the process of improving your law firm's performance. Improvement in one area will make it easier to improve the others. Your success will build on itself, and the evolution of your firm will be astounding. Just the momentum created by heading in the right direction will inspire you and your employees to create solutions never thought of before. Once your employees believe that you have a goal of making your firm the best it can be in all these areas, they will direct their efforts and performance to make it happen.

It is an amazing thing to see and experience when you *Run Your Firm Like a Business.*

APPENDIX 1
SAMPLE TELEPHONE INTAKE FORM—DIVORCE

1. Date: ________ Appt. Date & Time: __________

LEGAL NAME *Allow enough time to receive paperwork in mail

2. (L) ________ (F) ________ (MI) __

SPOUSE'S LEGAL NAME

3. (L) ________ (F) ________ (MI) __

QUOTED CONSULTATION FEE
$200.00 / $350.00

4. CLEAR CONTACTS

❑ OK
❑ Stop

5. Address: ________________
6. Cell Phone: ________ Home Phone: ________

Work Phone: ________ Other Phone: ________

7. Referral Source: ❑ Internet ❑ Personal ❑ Advertisement
8. Have you lived in Hawaii at least 6 months? Date arrived:

❑ Yes
❑ No

9. Does your spouse know that you are filing for divorce?

❑ Yes

❑ No

10. Does your spouse agree with everything?

❑ Yes

❑ No

11. Years married: ______ Date of marriage: ______

12. **Presently living together?* Separation date: ______

❑ Yes

❑ No

13. Is spouse a resident of Hawaii?

❑ Yes ❑ Oahu ❑ Outer Island

❑ No

14. **Spouse address:* ______

15. No. children: ___ Ages: ______ ___ #<23 in college full time: -

16. Any step-children: ❑ Husband ______

❑ Wife ______

17. Is there a TRO or is this a CPS case?

❑ Yes

❑ No

Any proceedings?

❑ Yes

❑ No

18. Is wife pregnant?

❑ Yes

❑ No

Is husband the father?

❑ Yes

❑ No

19. Has wife had a child during the marriage fathered by another man?

❑ Yes

❑ No

Is there a paternity judgment?

❑ Yes

❑ No

20.

❑ Advise Kids First filing fee is required (if children are involved)

21. Pre-nuptial?
    - ❑ Yes
    - ❑ No
22. Real estate (condos, empty lots, house)? ______________________
    - ❑ Yes
    - ❑ No
23. Own a business or securities? ______________________
    - ❑ Yes
    - ❑ No
24. Military service: Rank ________ Years in ________
    - ❑ Husband ❑ Retired
    - ❑ Wife
25. Do you have a Military Separation Agreement?
    - ❑ Yes
    - ❑ No
26. Retirement or Pension:
    - ❑ Husband ❑ Claim made ❑ Waived
    - ❑ Wife
27. Are you or is your spouse seeking alimony?
    - ❑ Yes
    - ❑ No
28. Agreed on Payment of Debts?
    - ❑ Yes
    - ❑ No
29. Agreed on Dividing Household and Personal Effects?
    - ❑ Yes
    - ❑ No

CLIENT'S CHIEF CONCERNS:

____

____

____

____

- ❑ WCB
- ❑ Send pkt
- ❑ Logged in New Contacts

Referred to __________

- ❑ Bring two pay stubs
- ❑ Paperwork must be filled out completely or appointment may have to be rescheduled. We want as much time as possible to spend on issues and concerns, not filling out paperwork.
- ❑ Bring consultation payment (exact amount)

Okay to mail documents to home address?

- ❑ Yes
- ❑ No

Mailing address: ____

We will call to confirm appointment. Okay to leave message?

- ❑ Yes
- ❑ No

On which phone: ______________________________

APPENDIX 2
SAMPLE LEGAL REPRESENTATION AGREEMENT

This Agreement confirms that LAW FIRM NAME HERE has been retained to represent you, the CLIENT, in your particular family law matter. This Agreement supersedes all prior agreements and understandings between us, and may only be modified in writing and signed by both parties. Once this Agreement is signed by both parties it is a binding agreement between us. **PLEASE READ CAREFULLY BEFORE SIGNING.**

1. THE CLIENT'S INFORMATION

In this Agreement, the words "you" and "your" refer to you the client.

Your Name: ______________________________

Address: __________________________

Date of Birth: __________ Social Security Number: ______________

CONTACT INFORMATION

Cellular Telephone: ____________Home: ____________

E-mail address: _______________ Fax Number: ____________

CHILDREN'S INFORMATION

Name: _______________

Birthdate: _______ Social Security Number: ________________

Name: _______________

Birthdate: _______ Social Security Number: ________________

Name: ____________________
Birthdate: _________ Social Security Number: ____________________
Name: ____________________
Birthdate: _________ Social Security Number: ____________________

2. THE LAW FIRM

In this Agreement, the words "we" and "us" refer to LAW FIRM NAME HERE (the "Firm"). You are hiring the Firm to provide legal assistance limited to: ______________________________________

THE FIRM'S ADDRESS AND CONTACT INFORMATION

LAW FIRM NAME HERE
A Professional Corporation
40 Anywhere Street, Suite 123
Anytown, Kansas 12345

Telephone: (555) 555–5555
Fax: (555) 555–5555
John Smith: jsmith@SmithLaw.com
Jane Jones: jjones@SmithLaw.com

3. THE OPPOSING PARTY

Your spouse, ex-spouse, or person with whom you have a conflict is:

Name: ____________________
Address: __________________

Date of Birth: _____________ Social Security Number: _____________
Telephone Number: _______________ Work number: ______________

OUR AGREEMENTS

4. WHAT YOU AGREE TO DO

As our client you agree to do all of the following:

a. Answer all our phone calls and letters promptly;
b. Call us only during normal business hours at our office, unless we make other arrangements or you have an emergency;

c. Supply us with needed information promptly. We will need to know all information about your and the opposing party's assets, debts, income and expenses;
d. Inform us of any new address or telephone numbers;
e. Come to our office at reasonable times, when requested;
f. Answer questions before trial, possibly at another lawyer's office;
g. Answer written questions (interrogatories) presented to you by the opposing party's attorney;
h. Appear in court whenever requested by the court. We will write you or call you about the dates and times of your court dates;
i. Testify in court;
j. Talk to us about your wishes and goals and assist in settling all or parts of your case;
k. Decide if a settlement is acceptable to you. While we may recommend a settlement, the final decision to settle is always yours, not ours. If you should choose not to settle your case, you can always have a judge make a decision;
l. Cooperate in processing your case;
m. Do whatever else is reasonably requested of you to do.
n. Pay additional amounts of retainer if requested by us (see Paragraph 7).

5. WHAT WE AGREE TO DO

a. OUR WORK IN GENERAL:

1. We will try to obtain a settlement of this matter in the most expedient manner possible. If this is not possible, we will start (or defend) a lawsuit to protect your interests.
2. At all times we will be ready to discuss settlement. In fact, we will always be looking for opportunities to settle when we think it would be wise to do so.
3. Our services may also involve:
    a. custody and visitation of children;
    b. child support;

c. claims for support;
d. division of property;
e. recovery of attorney's fees and costs if the law provides and the court approves a claim for the opposing party to pay for your fees. **Please understand that there is no guaranty that a claim for attorney's fees and costs will result in the court awarding you what you ask for.**

b. OUR WORK IN SOME DETAIL

Our services (which may be performed by one or more attorneys or a paralegal) may also involve:

1. Consulting with you in person and over the phone during normal business hours;
2. Speaking to others, as well as case-review meetings between our attorneys and paralegals;
3. Researching the law and investigating the facts in your case;
4. Giving you reports about important steps in the case;
5. Explaining the legal issues and the practical considerations in your case as well as its strengths and weaknesses;
6. Reviewing documents you and others have sent us;
7. Preparing a settlement agreement;
8. Preparing and filing all necessary court papers;
9. Preparing or responding to pre-trial requests for support, custody, visitation, and matters necessary to protect you, your interests, or your children;
10. Advising you when you are being questioned by the opposing party's lawyer;
11. Preparing other witnesses beside yourself who may be necessary or helpful in your case;
12. Hiring, at your expense, experts, and consulting with them about your case, your assets, and those of the opposing party;
13. Preparing for hearings and trial;
14. Conducting a hearing or trial on your behalf at court (this includes travel time to and from court);
15. Preparing a final decree for the judge to sign and preparing a closing letter advising you of important matters;

16. Handling post-trial activity at the trial court level until the final decree is signed by the judge.

6. WHAT WE ARE NOT AGREEING TO DO

a. We will have no duties after the final settlement or decision (including, but not limited to, the Divorce Decree, judgment, or order) is signed by the judge. If you or the opposing party subsequently decide to pursue post-judgment, enforcement or other issues, and we agree at that time to represent you in those matters, we will make a separate agreement from this agreement at that time.
b. We are **NOT** agreeing to take any appeal of this case to a higher court for you. If you decide to appeal this case (or if the opposing party decides to appeal), and we agree at that time to represent you on the appeal, we will make a separate agreement from this agreement at that time.
c. We are **NOT** agreeing to handle the following matters even though they involve you or your property:

1. Selling your home or other property;
2. Handling any other matter in any court other than Family Court;
3. Preparing your will;
4. Suing family corporations or other persons;
5. Defending a suit by a lender who may be foreclosing on your home;
6. Defending any other lawsuits by others against you.

d. Rendering tax, business or real estate advice. If you need this type of advice, we will hire experts with your permission or refer you to experts in the appropriate field.

7. PAYMENT TO LAWYER

a. You agree to pay this Firm for the time spent at the following rates. This Firm bills in increments of one-tenth of an hour.

- John Smith: $ 275.00 per hour
- Jane Jones: $ 200.00 per hour
- William Right: $ 185.00 per hour
- Paralegal: $ 100.00 per hour

b. You agree to reimburse (or advance if requested) the firm for the following costs:

- expert witnesses
- messenger service
- service of process
- witness fees
- filing fees
- photocopying
- long distance
- any other necessary costs
- investigators
- postage
- transcripts
- faxes

c. You agree to pay the Statements for Services Rendered (Invoice), or add to your retainer, if requested, within 10 days of the date of your receipt of these statements (invoices). If you do not, you will be charged simple interest on all amounts due at the rate of 1% per month (12% per year). You also authorize us to have any funds intended for you as part of the property settlement or division, **made payable to the Firm** should you still owe us any fees or costs **before you receive your settlement or division proceeds.** This applies to proceeds to be received not only from the opposing party but from third parties as well, such as escrow companies, pension plan administrators, etc.

d. Under certain circumstances, you may be charged a fixed rate or fee for preparation of computer-generated documentation that enables us to prepare documents at a fraction of the time it used to take. This firm has made, and continues to make, ongoing, substantial financial investments in computer hardware and software to enable us to compete with firms several times our size. The fixed-rate fee passes along to you the savings this investment has created.

e. In certain circumstances the law provides that one party should pay or contribute to the opposing party's attorney's fees. If we discuss the possibility that we may attempt to get the court to order that the opposing party do this, we also are informing you that there is **no guaranty** of this success. It all depends on how the judge sees the equity (fairness) in the case. Regardless of the judge's ruling, you still owe us the fees generated from this agreement.

8. ADVANCE PAYMENTS BY YOU

a. We are unable to predict how much time we will have to spend on your case and the amount of the expenses we incur on your behalf. Therefore, **WE CANNOT PREDICT THE AMOUNT OF YOUR FEE. As we have discussed, our time and expenses depend on a variety of factors over which we have no control. Such factors include how the opposing party or attorney behaves, and how much you or they will dispute any given issue in your case.**

b. You have deposited with us $ __ as an initial retainer (deposit against fees and costs) which we will deposit into our Clients' Trust Account. This is just an initial retainer amount and does not necessarily reflect what the total attorney's fees and cost will be in your case. Each month we will send you a detailed statement for services rendered indicating exactly the work we have performed and the expenses we have incurred. At that time we will withdraw the amount indicated in the statement from the Clients' Trust Account and pay (or reimburse) the Firm. Within fifteen (15) days of the date of this statement, you agree to deposit the amount billed in order to keep the retainer at the above-indicated amount. Should you fail to make this deposit within this fifteen (15) day period, you hereby authorize this Firm to charge a credit card or cards for this amount, designating the card numbers and expiration dates you have provided below. Your signing of this Agreement constitutes your continued authorization to charge said credit card or cards each and every month should you fail to deposit amounts billed to the trust account within fifteen (15) days of the date of your billing statements. As a courtesy to you, you will be informed by telephone of the amount and date of this transaction before it is charged.

c. There will also be times when we ask you to deposit more than this minimum amount into the Clients' Trust Account. This will be done when it becomes apparent that your case will require more work in the future than can be covered by the present retainer amount. (This typically happens when an issue that you thought was uncontested becomes contested, or when your case is set for trial by the opposing party or you.) You agree to deposit any additional amounts requested based upon our estimate of the work required.

d. Subject to subparagraph 8a above, if there is money left from your retainer after the final statement has been sent and all costs have been paid, we will REFUND the unused retainer to you.

9. TIME RECORDS

Everyone for whom you are responsible for paying hourly fees will be keeping time records for tasks accomplished. All time records billed to you will be contained in the detailed statement of services you receive each month. This Firm bills in increments of one-tenth of an hour.

10. TELEPHONE CALLS

Please understand that all telephone calls, no matter how brief, are billed at the hourly rate indicated in paragraph 7a. above.

11. WITHDRAWING BY LAWYER/ ATTORNEY'S CHARGING LIEN

You agree that if any of the following occur you will allow our withdrawal as your attorney from this matter and to give us security in the form of an Attorney's Charging Lien for any unpaid fees or unreimbursed costs we have incurred on your behalf:

a. you do not pay our bill on time;
b. you insist that we do something illegal or unethical;
c. you withhold or misrepresent anything to us, the opposing party, or to the court, or you tell us that you intend to do so;
d. you fail to answer our phone calls or letters;
e. you take a position which we find legally insupportable;
f. the Court allows this Firm to withdraw for any other reason.

12. NO GUARANTY

The result in your case will depend on many uncertain factors. One such factor will be how the judge (should this matter go to trial) weighs all the evidence and how he/she applies the wide discretion allowed to him/her by law. For this and many other reasons, no lawyer is able to guarantee the result in your case.

13. READ AND UNDERSTAND THIS AGREEMENT

I have requested that you take this Agreement home, read all of it and ask us all the questions you have until you understand it. **DO NOT SIGN THIS AGREEMENT UNLESS YOU UNDERSTAND ALL THE TERMS IN IT AND WISH TO HIRE THE FIRM UNDER ALL SUCH TERMS.**

14. COPY

After you and we sign this Agreement, we will provide you with a copy.

BY SIGNING THIS AGREEMENT, YOU AND THE FIRM AGREE TO ABIDE BY ALL ITS TERMS.

____

JOHN SMITH DATED

____

LAW FIRM NAME HERE

____

CLIENT DATED

RETURN THE ORIGINAL SIGNED COPY OF THE ENTIRE LEGAL REPRESENTATION AGREEMENT TO OUR FIRM. **Faxed or e-mailed copies are considered interim versions.**

CLIENT BILLING INFORMATION

(Law Firm Name Here Requires TWO Credit Cards On File)

I HEREBY AUTHORIZE THIS FIRM TO CHARGE THE FOLLOWING CREDIT CARDS, IN THE ORDER INDICATED BELOW, FOR AMOUNTS BILLED AND NOT PAID WITHIN FIFTEEN (15) DAYS OF THE DATE OF THE BILLING STATEMENT.

____

SIGNATURE OF CLIENT DATED

First Choice: *circle one* Visa MasterCard Discover

____

CREDIT CARD NUMBER

____

CODE #

____

EXPIRES

____

NAME AS IT APPEARS ON CREDIT CARD

Second Choice: *circle one* Visa MasterCard Discover

____

CREDIT CARD NUMBER

____

CODE #

____

EXPIRES

____

NAME AS IT APPEARS ON CREDIT CARD

BILLING ADDRESS OF CREDIT CARDS:

____

STREET ADDRESS, CITY & ZIP CODE

GUARANTOR BILLING INFORMATION

I HEREBY GUARANTY PAYMENT FOR THE FEES AND COSTS CHARGED PURSUANT TO THE ABOVE AGREEMENT. I HEREBY AUTHORIZE THIS FIRM TO CHARGE THE FOLLOWING CREDIT CARDS INDICATED BELOW FOR AMOUNTS BILLED AND NOT PAID WITHIN FIFTEEN (15) DAYS OF THE BILLING STATEMENT.

____

SIGNATURE OF GUARANTOR DATED

PRINT NAME OF GUARANTOR:

____

SOCIAL SECURITY NUMBER OF GUARANTOR:

____

DATE OF BIRTH OF GUARANTOR:

____

HOME ADDRESS OF GUARANTOR:

____

PHONE NUMBERS -

BUS: ____________________

HOME: __________________

CELL: ___________________

DRIVER'S LICENSE

STATE: __________

DRIVER'S LICENSE NO.: ______________________

First Choice: ***circle one*** Visa MasterCard Discover

____

CREDIT CARD NUMBER

____

CODE #

EXPIRES

NAME AS IT APPEARS ON CREDIT CARD

Second Choice: ***circle one*** Visa MasterCard Discover

CREDIT CARD NUMBER

CODE #

EXPIRES

NAME AS IT APPEARS ON CREDIT CARD

BILLING ADDRESS OF CREDIT CARDS:

STREET ADDRESS, CITY & ZIP CODE

APPENDIX 3
SAMPLE MISSION STATEMENT AND OPERATING VALUES

[NAME OF LAW FIRM HERE]
MISSION STATEMENT

The firm of **[NAME OF LAW FIRM HERE]** exists to bring understanding, stability, and resolution to our clients' lives in the difficult time surrounding a divorce. We accomplish these objectives in a timely manner by applying thorough legal and strategic analyses to their cases. The impact of our work is consistently communicated to build trust and reduce anxiety for our clients. We operate with integrity, guided by this mission and our operating values, to optimize performance and profit while creating a fulfilling and enjoyable work environment.

OPERATING VALUES:

- Constant improvement of communication skills and personal performance;
- Continuous education in the area of substantive and procedural law;
- Timely preparation and effective planning;
- Thorough research and continual follow through
- DWYSD (Do what you say you will do.)
- Doing what's right legally, ethically, and morally regardless of the consequences
- Preplanned initiative and solution-based thinking

APPENDIX 4
SAMPLE JOB DESCRIPTION: PARALEGAL OR LEGAL ASSISTANT

GENERAL RESPONSIBILITIES:

Assists attorneys in case and trial preparation, the organization of legal documents for various cases, legal researching, and drafting legal documents and conducting interviews with clients and witnesses. Assists attorneys in all aspects of case and file management and factual gathering.

SPECIFIC DUTIES:

1. Monitors discovery responses and requests for admissions, interrogatories, production of documents, and depositions (oral and written) to ensure appropriate action is taken on a timely basis.
2. Reads, analyzes, organizes, and arranges documents chronologically from various files and sources for future reference. Reviews and recommends necessary update actions on or for clients and attorneys.
3. Performs basic legal research as requested by attorneys including but not limited to retrieval of public information records and government records.
4. Reviews and follows trial calendar maintained by attorneys, paralegals, and intake coordinator for updating information and reminding self and attorney of important deadlines.
5. Develops an organizational system for deposition chronologies and summaries; and miscellaneous document preparation of charts and graphs; and organize and draft demonstrative exhibits as needed.

6. Drafts legal documents (i.e., correspondences, pleadings, forms, and requests and responses to interrogatories, production of documents, and admissions) for review and editing by supervising attorney. Performs typing, filing, and copying, scanning, and indexing assignments as required. Monitors document productions (incoming and outgoing documents).
7. Interviews clients and or witnesses for various cases (including case matters involving child custody, relocation, and TRO proceedings).
8. Trains and supervises administrative assistants regarding various litigation department procedures and administrative functions.
9. Assists attorneys in hearings, depositions, mediations, arbitrations, and trial preparation. (Coordinates supplies for attorneys. Identifies and labels exhibits; prepares adequate number of copies for distribution; and supplements and updates exhibit lists). Attends trials to assist attorney by providing or obtaining information attorney may need.

SPECIFIC SKILLS:

(Essential): Ability to analyze and prioritize workload. Must be able to work independently and use initiative to complete assignments. Must also be detail oriented with at least high school level English and speech skills. Good communication skills and demeanor required.

EDUCATIONAL REQUIREMENTS:

(Essential) High school degree or equivalent. Needs high school level reading and writing skills to process legal documents appropriately and prepare drafts of legal documents, short letters, and memos to and for attorneys. Also needs basic high school math to prepare and understand Property Division Charts, Income & Expense Statements, Asset & Debt Statements, Alimony Calculations, time sheets, and manual bills.

(Marginal) Paralegal certificate helpful.

EXPERIENCE REQUIREMENTS:

(Essential) Must have at least 1–2 years family/divorce law or civil litigation paralegal experience and at least clerical legal experience.

(Marginal) 2–3 years of family/divorce or litigation paralegal experience. 6 months to 1 year legal secretary experience or 6 months general office.

OFFICE MACHINE UTILIZATION:

(Essential) Office Machine Usage:

1. Computer: Frequent
2. Copier: Frequent
3. Fax: Frequent
4. Scanner: Frequent
5. Telephone: Frequent

OUTSIDE CONTACT:

Frequent contact with process servers, family court clerks, judges, court reporters, opposing counsel administrative assistants (to schedule depositions), and clerks of various state government and administrative agencies.

APPENDIX 5
PERFORMANCE EVALUATION

employee:
evaluator:
position held:
Time period: from to

Criteria	Rank	Comments	Goals
TECHNICAL SKILLS Capable of producing work effectively using willingness to continue to learn new the technology available. Takes initiative to maintain skills that are consistent with Firm standards.			
QUALITY OF WORK Is attentive to detail and accuracy, is committed to excellence, looks for improvements continuously, monitors quality levels, finds root cause of quality problems, owns and acts on quality problems.			
QUANTITY OF WORK Generates appropriate volume of work (billable and non-billable) within required timelines.			

Criteria	Rank	Comments	Goals
SERVICE ORIENTATION Practices and promotes service excellence. Recognizes the opportunity and provides clients exceptional, accurate, timely, and proactive assistance in a courteous and helpful manner.			
PROFESSIONALISM Projects a professional personal image and conducts self in a professional manner. Communicates effectively.			
INTERPERSONAL RELATIONS/TEAM SPIRIT Embraces cooperative practices to ensure effectiveness within team. Volunteers assistance and demonstrates a willingness to help others without being asked.			
INITIATIVE. Identifies opportunities and develops and implements solutions that contribute to the objectives of the team.			
JUDGMENT Demonstrates the ability to use sound judgment in decision making as it applies to his or her position.			
TIME MANAGEMENT Ability to effectively manage time, prioritizes works, and meets deadlines.			

Criteria	Rank	Comments	Goals
TIMEKEEPING Is diligent in tracking and logging time.			
DEPENDABILITY Demonstrates reliability through good attendance and punctuality.			

ABOUT THE AUTHOR

Throughout his 30-year legal career, Frank T. Lockwood has been a leader in innovation in the practice of law. He was the first lawyer mediator trained in the State of Hawaii, founded the Section on Alternative Dispute Resolution of the Hawaii Bar, and successfully advocated the use of mediation in Family Court cases. He designed and conducted the first mediation training for judges and lawyers. He pioneered the use of spreadsheets in alimony and property settlement cases in divorces and designed the first computerized family court forms program in Hawaii. Mr. Lockwood also installed computer systems into laws firms and trained lawyers and staff in the use of various software applications. He first conceived of the now successful Volunteer Settlement Master program in the First Circuit, State of Hawaii. After building his firm into a successful business, Mr. Lockwood sold his firm and retired from law practice at age 57 and currently resides in Durango, Colorado with his wife and dog. He frequently speaks to bar association conferences all over the country and consults with attorneys on re-thinking and re-designing more efficient systems for their law firms.

Mr. Lockwood can be contacted at flockwood@me.com, (970) 903-2138, or through his website LockwoodProfessionalDevelopment.com.

Throughout his 30-year legal career, Frank T. Lockwood has been a leader in innovation in the practice of law. He was the first lawyer mediator trained in the State of Hawaii, founded the Section on Alternative Dispute Resolution of the Hawaii Bar, and successfully advocated the use of mediation in Family Court cases. He designed and conducted the first mediation training for judges and lawyers. He pioneered the use of spreadsheets in alimony and property settlement cases in divorce, and designed the first computerized family court forms program in Hawaii. Mr. Lockwood also installed computer systems into law firms and trained lawyers and staff in the use of various software applications. He first conceived of the now successful Volunteer Settlement Master program in the First Circuit, State of Hawaii. After building his firm into a successful business, Mr. Lockwood sold his firm and retired from law practice at age 57. He now consults with attorneys on re-thinking and re-designing more efficient systems for their law firms.

Law/Reference

ISBN: 978-1-62722-222-8

57995

9 781627 222228

Price: $79.95
PC: 5150462

Defending Liberty
Pursuing Justice

Printed in the U.S.A.